SELLING FISH

SELLING FISH

~

J. H. HALL

STACKPOLE
BOOKS

Published by
STACKPOLE BOOKS
5067 Ritter Road
Mechanicsburg, PA 17055
www.stackpolebooks.com

Printed in the United States
10 9 8 7 6 5 4 3 2 1

First edition

Cover designed by Caroline M. Stover

Library of Congress Cataloging-in-Publication Data

Hall, J.H.
    Selling fish: stories from a fishing life / J.H. Hall.—1st ed.
        p. Cm.
    ISBN 0-8117-1535-3 (hard cover)
        1. Fisheries—Anecdotes. 2. Fishing—Anecdotes. 3. Hall, J.H. I. Title

SH331 .H24 2000
799.1—dc21   00-029729

"Selling Fish," "Preston," and "Catch and Remember" first appeared in the
In-Fisherman; "Guidance" first appeared in *Fly Rod and Reel*; "Slough
Fever" and "Fishing Partners" first appeared in *Fly Fishing News*; "Swim-
ming the Selway" first appeared in *Gray's Sporting Journal*.

For Preston and Evan

CONTENTS

Selling Fish

I come from fishing people. My grandfather, three great-uncles, several cousins, and a sister all fished or continue to fish the Chesapeake Bay commercially. Commercial fishing was my first ambition too.

From as far back as I can remember until I was about twelve, I spent a large part of each summer sitting spellbound on the bow of my cousin Hal's workboat, watching as he fished his traps. Each trap was like a deep, mysterious well, because we could not see the fish when we first pulled alongside, just a few crabs clinging to the sides of the net and sometimes a formation of stingrays circling the pound net. Then as the net was tightened, there would be a deep boil that barely reached the surface, then a dark cloud flecked with silver, and finally an eruption of fish—trout, spot, croaker, blues, bunkers, stripers, swell toads, oyster toads, eels, cobia. I was hypnotized by the fish then. I think I have been ever since.

A cousin, Steve, about my age, was equally affected, maybe worse, and when we were old enough we went into business for ourselves. Once we seined carp from a brackish pond, caught six in an afternoon. Another time we got a tip that eels were much in demand overseas. "The most expensive fish in the bay," Hal, our mentor, informed us. By nightfall we were in the eel business, handlining them from underneath Hal's dock, but it was literally a one-night stand. Once we fished out the locals, the ones that fed on dead soft crabs and fish scraps, it was over.

Two years later we were better organized, and now Steve owned a gill net. At night we would leave it along the bay shore to intercept the bottom feeders that moved in with the tide. Come morning we would haul it in, ice down our catch, and spend the rest of the day fishing the shallow coves that formed the shoreline of that farm. That was where the big croakers—jumbo hardhead—hung out. We would surround a likely spot with net, then thrash the water white with a tree limb, oar, prop wash, all the time watching the line of corks for the big fish to hit the net. For us it was almost as much fun as catching them on hook and line. In some ways better, because by the weekend we had over twenty dollars apiece.

I don't know exactly what happened after that. Time, I guess, or parental expectations, or peer pressure. In any case, by the time I took another crack at commercial fishing, twenty years had passed, and I was board certified in internal medicine. Those credentials, I soon learned, hurt my credibility with real commercial fishermen. Steve wandered even farther astray: He became a lawyer but remained a weekend gill netter, even now.

One sweltering summer morning in 1972, I was wrestling with a filthy gill net, trying to separate the few good fish from tangles of net, sea nettles, crabs, bunkers, and fish ruined by crabs. I heard a diesel engine of a workboat pull alongside and throttle down. Someone shouted, "When you going to go to work?"

I looked up and saw Jimmy Kelley, another cousin, a real commercial fisherman. I smiled and waved and went back to what I thought *was* real work. As he roared off after menhaden (which he froze and sold for crab bait; made a killing), I thought, "He oughta know better than that."

Even a distant cousin should have known our family was famous for turning out well-educated fishermen. Uncle Eugie came within a thesis of a Ph.D. from Columbia but spent the best years of his working life on the water. My sister has a degree from William & Mary and takes graduate courses in archeology. We Halls aren't dumb; we just like to fish. (Most of us. It skipped my father and brother, but those of us afflicted are severely so.)

I gill netted all that summer and into the fall, when the weather settled, the water cleared, the sea nettles disappeared, and the striped bass schooled up to leave the bay. Hal came out of semiretirement to fish with me, and that probably accounted for our success. One day, one dead calm, November morning, we caught over a thousand pounds of striped bass. We just followed the birds and, when we caught up to them, ran out our net and waited. As we pulled it in, sportfishermen trolled around us, staring. By midmorning the skiff was riding low, loaded with pure stripers up over our ankles. Riding in, we were pleased with ourselves, more pleased than we would have been if we had known those were the last of the striped bass for a very long time.

The next spring, using larger mesh net, we caught more from the same school year, but that was the end of it. That summer, I put away my gill net and joined a group of internists on the other side of the Bay. That career lasted exactly one year longer than my career as a commercial fisherman. Then I put away my stethoscope, packed up my typewriter, and moved to Maine. Before I left I bought a fly rod, because I thought that was the only type of fishing that was done in Maine.

For years after I moved to Maine, I wrote and fished and fished and wrote, but I never wrote about fishing. What did I know about fishing? I was a novice then, and even now am certainly no expert. But finally I decided I did know a couple of things. One thing I learned was that the flow of a river could exert as strong an influence on a person as the rise and fall of a tide, that a pond had its own rhythm too, and that in the long run it didn't really matter whether you took your fish with handline, gill net, or fly rod.

Of course, it matters in terms of how we affect the resource, but not at all in terms of how the resource affects us. Whether it's trout rising to a mayfly, bluefish chasing bunkers, or the entire contents of a pound net slowly forced to the surface—if there's magic in any of it, it's in the fish and where they live and how they suddenly, remarkably reveal themselves to us and how we, the afflicted, react.

So now, when I write about fishing, that is what I write about—the pull of fishing in all its forms, the undertow. Occasionally I sell a piece. When that happens, I see myself continuing in the tradition of my grandfather, great-uncles, and cousins. The way I see it, I'm still selling fish.

Preston

My older son, Preston, caught his first fish when he was five years old, a two-pound smallmouth on a popping bug dragged behind my canoe. He caught several other fish that season, nice fish. Once we found smallmouths feeding on a mayfly hatch, and he took three good fish in a row. He had fun, and I though he was hooked, but I was wrong. He threw that hook, and his interest went the other way.

When he was nine, he pulled me off a school of feeding bluefish in the Chesapeake Bay. Moments after I had removed two fish from his line, he reeled in and said he was bored and wanted to go home. "You just caught two fish at one time!" I said. "And you're bored?"

"They were small," he said.

They *were* small, but he wasn't so big himself. I looked at the fish still boiling the water a few yards away, at the frantic gulls, and back at my son, my firstborn, my beloved—at least I thought he was my son—now reclining in the bow. I cranked the engine, opened the throttle, and ran straight inshore. I didn't bother docking;

I just ran the bow aground. He hopped out, and I shoved off and headed back to where the fish had been, a tranquil spot now marked by slick water and resting gulls. The fish were gone. Still, that was a better place for me to be than onshore with him.

The next summer, on a remote trout pond in Maine, brook trout rose so steadily that Preston hooked one on his backcast. Then he handed me the rod. His arm was tired. "Are you sure?" I asked. "You may never have another chance like this."

He was sure. So while I fished, he paddled and netted and unhooked what I caught. I noticed that he enjoyed handling the fish, studying them, holding them first one way, then the other in the sunlight. A good sign, or so I thought.

That winter, casting from a coral beach on Cayman Brac, he caught three yellow jacks and a three-pound bonefish that fought like it was trying to work its way into a higher weight class. "Now admit it," I said as we were walking up the beach. "That was fun, wasn't it?"

He shrugged. "Sort of," he said, "but I've had more fun playing video games."

Any fisherman will recognize that remark as grounds for infanticide, but I refused to let it rile me. I knew he meant it as a joke, so I laughed, but I could see real fatigue in his face. His Norwegian ancestry hadn't prepared him for the tropics. He was hot and tired now, and ten minutes after the fact, that bonefish was history.

Later that day, three hours after losing a fish about the size of the one he caught, I was still trembling. Such speed and power! It seemed physically impossible that a fish that size could be so strong, and equally unlikely that anyone could recover from catching one in a matter of minutes. I knew then that nothing that swam on the face of this earth would turn my son into a fisher-man. I think I'd known it all along, but now, finally, I accepted it.

In the interest of salvaging our relationship, we made a deal. In the mornings I would fish. He could come or not, as he wished. In the afternoons we would do something together. Mostly what we did was snorkel.

Our first time out, walking across the hot sand to the water, Preston looked up at me, no more Mr. Wise Guy now, but a ten-year-old with a troubled look on his face. "Are you a little worried?" he said.

I knew what he meant. Neither of us had ever done this before, and there was a lot of water out there, and we didn't know exactly what was in it. "A little bit," I said, "but we'll take it slow and easy."

We waded out in fins and mask, then under. What had been a shimmering blue mirror became a window to another world, a world of fish—cherub, angel, butterfly, squirrel, wrasse, razor, trigger. We didn't know their names then, but it didn't matter. We paddled along, pointing things out to each other. Preston's eyes were wide now, his gestures jerky and excited.

There was an undertow that carried us toward a dock, beneath which thick schools of fish hovered in the shade. We let the current carry us around the dock into milkier, murky water and abruptly found ourselves within a few yards of a four-foot barracuda. That very morning our guide had entertained us with a barracuda story, which I was now sorry I remembered in such detail, right down to the number of stitches it had taken to close the wound. (A hooked fish had wrapped itself around a man's leg. Chasing the fish, the barracuda bit the man. At least, we thought he was chasing the fish.) Our barracuda held motionless near the bottom as we paddled back upcurrent. The fish's eyes seemed to follow us, possibly an illusion, but the hot sand still felt good to our feet.

"He probably wouldn't have bothered us anyway," I said. "He was probably more afraid of us than we were of him, but what do you say we try it further up the beach?"

"That sounds like a *great* idea," Preston said. His vulnerability becomes him, endears him to me in a way his video game remarks do not. We're a team again. The barracuda has brought us back together. God bless barracuda, and to hell with bonefish. For now.

Up the beach there is coral and new species of fish and, to keep us honest, more danger: a rock scorpionfish, a small spotted moray, stinging coral, and a huge, though harmless (we think) spotted eagle ray that swoops and circles like an enormous bird of prey. Afterward we are both giddy and tired. This is better than a video game, or maybe it's like being inside one. But two more afternoons of that, and we are ready for bigger and better things. We're ready for the other side of the island.

There's no beach on the other side. It is all coral and drops off to twenty feet or more within a few yards of shore. A small lagoon has been hacked out of the coral. We clamber down, ungainly until we're in the water. The lagoon is clogged with fish. An iridescent curtain of minnows parts to let us pass, then closes behind us. The other fish—queen angel, parrot, others we don't recognize—are larger here and nibble at the coral. Preston reaches out to touch a blue tang—I've seen him reach for our cat the same way—but the fish darts off.

We move out of the lagoon into open, deeper water. I dive toward the bottom, turn, and look back up at my son, who hovers several feet above me as if in flight. He smiles around his mouthpiece. We cruise through a forest of coral and sea fans, discover new species of fish, each seemingly more colorful than the last.

It is all very beautiful, but eventually I get tired and cold. Also, there's only so much fish beauty I can take before I start thinking in terms of hook size and leader strength. Soon I touch Preston on the shoulder. We pull back our masks and tread water. "Are you about ready to go in?" I ask.

"What? No!" he says. "We just got here. We can't go in now."

I recognize the look, the tone of voice. It is mine on the Chesapeake. I make an offer: I'll get out and sit onshore. He can swim in the lagoon where I can watch him. This doesn't faze his disappointment. So I throw in a return trip tomorrow.

"And the day after that," he says.

"All right. All right." We turn and swim slowly back.

I warm myself in the sun and watch as Preston porpoises about in the lagoon. He pauses now and then to throw back his mask and relate some new discovery. He is hooked good this time; he is hooked himself. It's funny, but the same tackle that connects me to fish, bonds me even, separates him. Eliminate the tackle and he is as exhilarated by fish as I am.

I'm glad. It's what I wanted to happen, but I know how these things work, how one thing leads to another. As I sit there in the warm sun watching him, I find myself calculating the cost of scuba gear, and I feel a twinge of nostalgia for the good old days when a handful of quarters would buy him off for hours.

Guidance

IN MANY WAYS A FLYFISHERMAN'S FIRST GOOD BONEFISHING GUIDE is like his first girlfriend. The same adolescent hazards pertain: fear of embarrassment and failure. In each instance there is a rite of passage, after which life is never quite the same.

Carlos Marin was not my first bonefishing guide. In previous years, I'd used guides on Cayman Brac, Little Cayman, and briefly in the Florida Keys. But somehow those relationships didn't click. In Florida, it was a lack of fish, compounded by our guide's disposition. My fishing partner and I had booked him at the last minute, pulling him away from his daughter's school play, which she had been rehearsing for weeks. Apparently his contract with the marina required him to take us, but that didn't mean he had to like it. His absence from her play cast a pall over the afternoon. In retrospect, we all would have been better off at the play. Our guide would have been happier, and we would have saved money and seen exactly the same number of fish.

On Cayman Brac the fishing was ruined by a philosophical difference: I was determined to catch bonefish on flies. The guide,

Mr. Bodden, was of the opinion that a bonefish would not take a fly unless it was first feeding on crushed minnows. He scoffed at my flies—Crazy Charlie, Bonefish Special, Mother of Epoxy. "No, they're no good," he said.

He believed so fervently in the effectiveness of minnows that he tossed a handful to the only tailing fish we saw all week. When the fish fled in a cloud of murky water, he offered that as evidence not of a failure of his method, but of the futility of fishing for bones in such shallow water. His method was to chum them in depths of two to three feet, where I would cast to the feeding school—with a fly, though he would have preferred a minnow. It was more like bluefishing than bonefishing, but at least I felt for the first time the speed and power of a bonefish and experienced that mind-boggling incongruity between size and strength. I also learned to tie a reasonable crushed minnow imitation.

The next year, on Little Cayman, I had more success fishing alone without a guide. I seemed to be better at following my own instincts than someone else's instructions. And I like to walk and wade alone. I do not like people reading over my shoulder, books or bonefish flats.

So the following year in Belize, I did not hire a guide in advance. Instead, I rented a four-wheeler, which I used to explore the island for wadable flats that I could fish alone. I let my thirteen-year-old son Preston drive. When I tossed him the keys, he looked at me in joyful disbelief. He'd never driven a motorized vehicle before. When, on a straight, empty stretch of road, I said to open it up, he was even more incredulous. Normally he was bucking at the reins; now suddenly without reins, he was tentative. He toyed with the throttle, slowly opening it bit by bit. He didn't realize that while he was testing the machine's throttle, I was checking his brakes. It was reassuring to see his natural restraints at work.

We saw many interesting sights that afternoon—huge lizards, strange birds, the funky sights of San Pedro, but only one very small wadable flat. The rest were soft. That evening, fly rod in hand, I walked down the beach to the one wadable flat. En route, I passed a sign on the beach I hadn't seen before because we'd gone by road. The sign said, "Flyfishing—Tarpon Bonefish Permit." Staked a few yards offshore was a small skiff with a pushpole protruding from the stern. Away from the water was a cinderblock bungalow, an American car, and a man washing it. He was small, lean, with coppery skin and lips cracked from the sun. I said hello. "Is that your sign?" I asked. He said it was. He continued washing his car. No hard sell and he took care of his equipment. I asked about the type of fishing he did. He said his fishermen cast flies to sighted fish. "No chum?" He seemed offended. I changed the subject. "What flies do you like?" "Crazy Charlie is good," he said.

Then he put down his rag, came over, and inspected my rod, a nine-foot graphite for a seven-weight. He wiggled it and examined the reel. "How much backing?" I told him. I asked if he was free in the morning. He said he was. Still, I was not ready to commit. "I'm going out and try this flat," I said. "I'll check with you when I come back." "OK." He resumed washing his car. I was back within the hour.

In the morning the wind was from the southeast, too hard. "How long is this wind going to last?" I asked. Carlos said that when he was washing his car yesterday, he heard the lizards cheep. "When the lizards cheep like that," he said, "it means one wind is going to stop and another is going to come. This is the one that has come." "But how long is it going to last?" I asked. "That I cannot say."

It lasted three days. It blew hardest on day two, but it was on day one that it had its most devastating effect. On day one it was a member of a conspiracy of elements—wind, nerves, inexperience—that ruined two hours of fishing. By nine-thirty I'd had good chances on at least a dozen tailing bonefish, and I had not hooked a fish. Not one. My casts were too long, too short, too hard; the cadence of stripping was all wrong. By nine-thirty it was very quiet in Carlos's boat. Carlos was standing beside me on the bow, leaning on the pushpole, looking quite dejected.

I wasn't feeling so well myself. I could feel the ego preparing to make a great plunge into a pool of self-recriminations. Somehow, at the last minute, it righted itself and allowed me to make a rather sensible analysis of the situation: this was hard fishing under the best of circumstances; these were not the best of circumstances; I was new at this, and the lessons of Cayman Brac had little carryover value; I had not touched a fly rod in five months; and I did have some ability with a fly rod, and I was capable of learning. Given the same number of opportunities for the rest of the morning, I would connect. I *would*.

I patted Carlos on the back. "Don't get so discouraged," I said. "I'll get the hang of this. We'll do all right. You just keep showing me the fish."

"OK," he said, but he did not sound convinced.

But, in fact, we did do OK, and by noon we had caught four fish, not large, "average sized bones," he called them. Even that was generous, but the size didn't matter. At least we had caught something. Carlos had found them; I had seen them, cast to them, hooked them, fought them; and Carlos had landed them. The guide-client relationship had been consummated. I signed up for three more days, all he had available.

San Pedro, on the island of Ambergris Cay, is two villages in one, two cultures. To the east, along the beach and the lagoon, are hotels, gift shops, dive boats, windsurfers, jet skis. The back side, the west, is a fishing village, a poor fishing village, with ramshackle housing and the rubble and litter of real lives. I was glad the bonefishing lay to the west, because the bonefishing did not feel like "vacation." It felt like "real life," the center of life around which all else revolved. I had the same feeling each morning as we rode out to the bonefish flats, through the narrow mangrove-choked channel, then out onto the shallows, sun rising behind us, surprised birds blossoming all around, and who knew what ahead. It was not a fleeting sensation, but one that grew more insistent every morning, until by week's end it had taken on words: "more time in skiffs, less time on shore." Not a promise or a resolution, but the solution to a problem I hadn't even known existed but that my mind apparently had been working on behind the scenes all along. In fishing circles these epiphanies fall under "personal growth."

On day two I caught five fish, missed four, and was the recipient of one pat on the back, one "good job," and one happy profanity when a long, last-ditch cast to a trio of departing fish landed miraculously on target. "Shit," Carlos said as the lead fish turned, took, felt the hook, and then transformed my reel into a small musical instrument. But on this occasion Carlos's voice, its spontaneity, its pitch was more pleasing to the ear than the reef's song.

On day three I caught another five fish, missed others, but this morning there were few compliments and few comments on obvious mistakes. It wasn't necessary. By now he knew my limitations. My major one, the one most frustrating to us both, was my inability to see the fish. If I could see them clearly, I could usually get the fly there, but too often he would point to fish, and I would see only an amorphous mix of glare and mottled water. "How can you not see the fish when they are *right there?*" I couldn't answer. Then, out of the impenetrable watery haze, fish would emerge into my field of vision. There had to be more to this than savvy. "Let me see your glasses," I said. I put them on and saw a different world. Carlos's glasses had brown lenses. Through them the flats were not nearly so lovely as seen through my own bluish green tinted prescriptions. Passing clouds were like patches of rust, but by God you could see. It was like looking at an X-ray of the flats.

Here was a patch of turtle grass and there was a fish, and never should the two be confused. I was hoping he would like my glasses as much as I liked his, that he would overlook the refractive error and be seduced by the lovely colors. No such luck. He took one look through mine and handed them back in disgust. "I don't like that color." And neither, anymore, did I.

At exactly quitting time, high noon, the visibility issue came to a very satisfying conclusion. Carlos was slowly poling us off the flats into somewhat deeper water, which through my glasses appeared bottomless and the color of turquoise. I was mesmerized by the color, and the warmth of the sun, and the soft breeze. Fish seemed out of the question. Then Carlos interrupted my reverie. "There's a bunch of fish you'll see," he said. And so I did. A school of about a dozen was hovering not on the bottom, but just beneath the surface, the fish's outlines dark, gray, distinct, like zinc on turquoise. The school was directly downwind and gave me my best fish of the day, like a parting gift, a donation to the visually impaired.

Day four began with the same sort of generosity as day three had ended, even more so. There was no wind, and we had three good fish in less than an hour. Then something happened. I'm not sure exactly what, but the next three hours were a reprise of the early hours of day one. I couldn't do anything right. I made sloppy casts; I broke fish off; I failed to set the hook, couldn't see the fish. It wasn't all my own doing. Some of it was bad luck, a fly simply pulling out of an apparently well-hooked fish; a good fish finding and wrapping the only mangrove within a hundred yards; a fish sighted, hooked, landed, turning out to be, not a bonefish, but a shad. "Damn," I said, when I saw it was the "wrong" species.

None of this bothered Carlos in the least. He took it all in stride. When the hook fell out, he shrugged and said, "That is nothing. It happens all the time." When the fish wrapped the mangrove, he reminded me that just the day before I had said how nice it was the fish never wrapped the mangroves. Now he seemed pleased that one had. His eyes said, "Better to lose the fish than lose respect for the fish. Any fish." He handled the shad as gently and respectfully as if it had been a trophy bone. He unhooked it and held it in the sunlight and admired it. "Nice, isn't it," he said. I said, "Yeah, right, of course it is." To show my heart was in the right place I took a picture of the shad. "I still can't help but be disappointed," I said, as I put the camera down. Carlos released the fish and looked up at me with what I believe was pity. "Poor gringo," his eyes said, "poor impoverished gringo, who can only like one type of fish."

Still I kept screwing up, and each screwup left me angrier. By noon, quitting time, I was as dejected as Carlos had been that first morning. We had come full circle. This time *he* patted *me* on the back. "Maybe you are just tired," he said. "I'm not tired," I said. "I'm pissed." Again he looked at me with pity. "Poor gringo. Fishing makes him angry."

I sat down and looked around at the enormous expanse of flats; the patterns of blues and greens and whites; the wading birds; mangroves; the blue sky and the scattered passing clouds. If I was angry in the midst of such plenty, then I really hadn't learned much about bonefishing. I may have learned a few things about how and where to cast, how to strip the fly, play the fish, and so on, but those were the lessons of basic literacy. There was more to it than that. There was an attitude, a state of mind one needed. I can not accurately describe it, because I have never been there. I operated on either side of it, swinging wildly from one extreme to the other, from insecurity to overconfidence with no stops in between. But I have seen irrefutable evidence of this attitude on Carlos's face, in the pleasure he takes in fish, in all fish.

I seriously doubt that this state of mind can be acquired in the way that we might acquire another piece of equipment. Possibly it can be absorbed over time. Time, the great enemy of bonefishing. More so even than money. Money is an obstacle. Money can be rationalized. More to the point, money can be borrowed, quietly with no one being the wiser. Time requires a public commitment. Time implies a seriousness of purpose, and people serious about fishing are generally considered not to be serious people. Unless, of course, they make a living at it. Then we all envy and look up to them, and wonder why the hell we didn't think of it earlier, before we had committed ourselves to the stock market or medicine.

Carlos said many rich people, many doctors, come to Belize to fish, and sometimes they leave him flies and other pieces of equipment. Some even leave their fishing rods, expensive graphite fly rods. I wondered why. As a tip? Money would make a better tip, and how much fly-fishing gear can Carlos use?

In retrospect, I think it is so they can leave a part of themselves there, where they feel they belong and long to be. So that when they are back in New York, or Seattle, or Maine, they will know that a part of themselves is alive and well and *fishing* in Belize.

One thing to remember when saying good-bye to guides: They always mean more to you than you do to them. It has to be that way. We have—what?—a handful of guides in a lifetime, *if* we're lucky. They have hundreds of clients. With them, it's always easy come, easy go. So there's no point getting emotional with your good-byes, no point wondering, "Was it as good for him as it was for me? Will he remember me a year from now?" It wasn't and he won't, and there's really nothing to say when you leave except "See you later." Anyway, that's all I said. Then I dumped the contents of one fly box into Carlos's palm and headed back up the beach.

Croakers, Toads, and Rock

IN OUR FAMILY ALBUM THERE'S A FADED BLACK AND WHITE PHOTO taken aboard the workboat *Mary Virginia* in the early fifties. In the foreground I am holding a "jumbo" hardhead, also known as croaker, that must have weighed four or five pounds.

In the background Hal stands with one hand on the tiller, staring off into the distance. Uncle Eugie, standing next to Hal with his hands tucked inside his waders, looks amused, as he usually did. (And why not? He'd beat the system; he'd escaped from the workaday world of Norfolk, where he'd served as school principal, and returned to the world he loved.)

Uncle Harry, jimmy-jawed, already frail, was scowling. Probably Hal hadn't tied the skiff properly to the stern cleat, or maybe he was towing it too close to suit Harry, or not close enough. Harry was a demanding father—a family trait. It would take more than a boatload of hardhead to make him overlook the flaws in that boy's technique.

For a ten-year-old, I looked pretty serious myself, but I *know* I was happy, because my feet were firmly planted in a pile of fish, my hands were on a fish, and I was on the Chesapeake with Harry, Eugie, and Hal. At least for that one glowing moment, all the ingredients of happiness were in place.

A croaker is called that because out of the water it makes a deep croaking noise, and it's called a hardhead because—no surprise here—it has a hard head, with sharp gill plates that make handling them without gloves tricky, especially in a gill net. By either name, for years they were the most valuable fish in the Bay. Their moist white meat made superb table fare, and croaker were firm and didn't spoil as fast as spot or trout. Our family's most lucrative day ever came from a huge catch of croaker on the Great Wicomico River before my time. They are also good sport on hook and line, bottom feeders that bite readily and pull hard. They're a ruggedly handsome fish as well, somewhat resembling a redfish, but not quite as sleek. All in all, there's nothing not to like about a croaker, but when their numbers crashed, there was no great outcry from commercial or sportfishermen. Sportfishing wasn't the big industry on the Bay then, and commercial fishermen knew that fish populations always ran in cycles. When one species declined, another often flourished. Spot and croaker seemed to have a reciprocal relationship, their populations seesawing back and forth.

A few years later the numbers of swell toads, also known as blowfish, dropped, and once again hardly anyone noticed. The only person I ever heard lament the decline of the swell toads was a man called "Lappa Dick," a slightly tongue-tied fish buyer at Little Bay, where Hal sold his fish. One hot summer day, in the early sixties, Lappa Dick asked when Hal was going to "bwing me anudder load a' toads." Hal just laughed, not because of how Lappa Dick talked, but because Lappa sounded irritated, as if Hal had some control over what species swam into his nets, as if Hal was just being contrary by not catching toads.

Except for that conversation, I doubt I would have noticed either that the toads' numbers were down. Swell toads are a funny-looking fish; you aren't apt to see one mounted on anyone's wall. They're boxy, with gnarly brown and yellow splotched sides, eyes like the headlights of an old Austin Healey, and rabbitlike front teeth. They'll take bait, but they don't fight much. They just sort of twitch at the end of the line, as if more puzzled by the hook than seriously upset. Skinned and served as "Chicken of the Sea," they're said to be good eating, though personally I have never eaten one. But I remember Lappa Dick's remark because, homely as they were, swell toads were always a special fish for me, because my grandfather used to blow them up like balloons, or at least I thought he did.

When I was just a tyke, my grandfather would take me and my brother out to bottom-fish with handlines and hunks of hard crab. When he caught a swell toad, he'd hold it to his mouth, put his lips just behind the pectoral fin, and huff and puff, and the fish's white, sandpaper-textured belly would swell with air until there was nothing fishlike left, just those strange eyes and teeth and a twitchy little tail attached to a leathery white ball. I would laugh, and grandfather would toss the toad back into the water, where the top-heavy fish would tip over, deflate, and slowly swim away. To this day I don't know for sure if you can actually inflate one that way. I've kissed a fish or two, but I've never put my lips to a swell toad or even been seriously tempted. I do know that you don't need to blow them up; they'll inflate themselves if you tickle their bellies or just hold them out of the water for a while. (I suppose it's a protective mechanism, but what's the point of being able to inflate after you're out of the water? It's too late.)

I remember times when the *Mary Virginia* would be so full of swelled toads that she looked to be carrying not fish, but volley-balls. Then, just like that, the toads were gone. Believe me, there was no great hue and cry, no "Protect the Toads" T-shirts, no demands for shorter seasons or tighter limits. Except for Lappa Dick's remark, nothing but silence (and maybe a sigh of relief from Hal's hired hands, who had to do the skinning, and it wasn't piecework either; they got paid by the week).

But a few years after that, the striped bass numbers crashed, and all hell broke loose. Because striped bass, known locally as rock, are *not* a funny-looking fish. They are silvery and sleek, with elegant black lines down each side like racing stripes. At times they feed on the surface on schools of menhaden beneath flocks of frenzied, screaming, diving gulls. And they'll take artificial lures, spoons, and bucktails and therefore are a favorite of sportfishermen, who soon came to think of striped bass as their own private species.

Commercial fishermen liked them too. The striped bass's dense white meat is delectable. In our family, rock was a "baking fish," a high compliment shared by buck shad, gray trout, and practically no other species. A load of striped bass always brought a high price. Fact was, everybody loved striped bass. And ironically in those not-so-distant but seemingly innocent days, most people loved commercial fishermen too. Their independent spirit, their rich traditions and quaint ways, their lore and language inspired several books. Museums commemorated the tools of their trade, the various styles of their handsome boats.

But when the stripers disappeared, commercial fishermen suddenly went from role models to plunderers and pillagers of the Bay, as if they were to blame rather than the newcomers with their big houses, polluting septic tanks, heavily fertilized lawns, and asphalt driveways. Even though commercial fishing may have been *a* factor in the striped bass's decline, it certainly wasn't the only one, and I took the criticism of those people personally, because I knew how much the commercial fishermen in my family loved that Bay and everything that lived therein. For those people to be criticized by newly anointed conservationists in the form of "come hithers" and sportfishermen seemed grossly unfair. It still does.

The first conservationist I ever saw in action on the Chesapeake was Otha, a black man who worked for Hal for many years.
While Hal and whoever else was helping would bail the good fish,
those big enough to sell, into the *Mary Virginia,* Otha would bail
the little fish overboard. This was long before catch and release was
popularized. Otha would even free the fish that got trapped along
the gunwale, including the lowly chokefish, which in the old days
served as trotline bait, but then was of no use to anyone. And they
weren't easy to pick up, either; they're flat like small flounder.
They would stick to the gunwale like placemats. But Otha
patiently, sometimes using his fingernails, would unstick them and
toss them overboard. I never even asked him why. The gentle way
he handled them, handled every fish, seemed answer enough.

I don't think Otha would have understood that to some people
he was the enemy of the Bay. For that matter, I doubt he would
have liked me calling him a conservationist. Otha was a waterman,
plain and simple. So were Harry, Eugie, and Hal. Being a waterman, putting food on people's tables, didn't need to be defended,
because it wasn't a crime. As Hal used to remind us, no less than
four of Jesus' disciples were commercial fishermen. If commercial
fishermen were good enough for Jesus Christ, Hal said, they darn
well ought to be good enough for people from Connecticut.

The good news now is, the Bay is showing signs of life again.
The striped bass are making a comeback. The exact reasons are no
clearer than the reasons for their disappearance. Reduced pollu-
tion, tighter limits, or even natural cycles may all play a role.
Whatever the reason, their numbers are now sufficient to support
a short commercial season. Much to the dismay of sportfishermen,
of course.

Small croaker are back in good numbers also, and I'm told that
spot and trout are picking up as well. No word yet on swell toads,
but then their return is not likely to make headlines anyway.

Scales

MY COMMERCIAL FISHING BACKGROUND HAS INSTILLED IN ME A very conservative approach to weights and measures. When fish are bought and sold by weight, every ounce matters. And a fraction of an inch can mean the difference between a legal and an illegal crab. When I took up freshwater sportfishing, I took a similar approach to fish measurements and naively assumed others did as well.

In my fishing diary, I meticulously recorded trout lengths to the nearest half inch. During my bass fishing apprenticeship, I carried an accurate set of scales in my canoe and carefully weighed and measured every bass I caught. Soon I had collected enough data that I no longer needed the scales. My rod was calibrated in inches. I could lip the fish, measure it against my rod, and have a very reasonable idea of its weight.

Gradually I met other fishermen; we talked, and to my chagrin I learned they invariably caught larger fish than I did. At first it didn't bother me. I was new to freshwater fishing and to fly fishing. Probably when I got more experience, I'd catch bigger fish too. Initially it didn't occur to me that there might have been another explanation for the discrepancy in fish size.

The first clue came one summer in the early eighties on David Pond, where we'd rented a camp. One morning an excited fifteen-year-old boy came running over from the next cabin, holding a nice smallmouth he'd caught while fishing with his father. He *knew* the fish weighed three pounds—his father said so—but he wanted to see if it might weigh even more.

I measured the fish at fifteen inches, a male, not much belly. "That's a nice fish," I said. "But it won't go three pounds."

"It's at least three," the boy insisted.

Reluctantly I weighed the fish. One and a half pounds.

"There's something wrong with those scales," he said. "I know it weighs three pounds."

"Look," I said, "that's a nice fish, no matter what it weighs. But a smallmouth usually won't go three pounds until it's over seventeen inches long."

The kid wasn't buying it. That was a three-pound fish, because his dad said it was. And his father had seen another fish that very morning that would've gone seven pounds! I was so touched by the young man's faith in his father, and his love of fishing, that I didn't bother arguing.

But after that episode, I became a bit skeptical of other people's catches. Whenever someone would talk of weight and length of fish, I would ask, as nonthreateningly as possible, "What sort of scales do you use? Do you have a separate tape measure or one mounted on the rod?" I was careful to use the same tone of voice, the same inflections—innocent, naiflike curiosity—as when I inquired about lure selection or rod choice. I was new to the sport and just trying to learn. I *was.*

Almost without fail, the response would be, "I didn't actually weigh him, but when you've caught enough, you can tell."

"Oh, I see." And I did see, and what I saw was, other people's fish were bigger than mine because they never measured them. And maybe I shouldn't have measured them either. I once had a guide tell me, "Measuring a fish insults the fish." His point is well taken: Size is not the true measure of a fish. But there is such a thing as science, and sadly for fishing romantics, science involves numbers, data.

In those days I kept a diary for Inland Fisheries and Wildlife. At the end of every season, I submitted my statistics, numbers of fish caught, size, species, location, and fishing method. I took my responsibility seriously and tried to make sure my numbers were accurate. Inaccurate optimistic estimates could easily have misled the biologists into thinking the fishery was healthier than it actually was. Deterioration of the resource could have been ignored. In that situation, I owed it to the fish to tell their true size, same as a doctor owes it to his patient to record an accurate blood pressure, not what the doctor wishes it were because he was attempting to control it. Therefore, I continued to take a hard line on data and to believe that I stood for truth, justice, and a healthy fishery. Then along came Conor.

On my younger son, Evan's, ninth birthday, a group of his friends came for the day. Serious, dark-haired, dark-eyed Conor asked if I would take him fishing. Would I ever! (It's so strange: I'm convinced there's a fishing gene, but it cruelly leapfrogs whole generations, leaving fathers with nonfishing sons and vice versa.)

We took the canoe; I paddled while Conor trolled a Mepp's spinner, occasionally casting to a dock or log. Soon he hooked a spunky largemouth near a partially submerged dock. The fish jumped—giving me a good look; it was about ten inches, less than a pound—and then dove. Conor reeled hard, maybe too hard. The next time the fish jumped, it threw the lure. We didn't stay long, and that was the only fish he hooked, but at least we had a little action, and there were no major accidents, no bug bites, no self-inflicted wounds, and we hadn't capsized; so I considered the trip a success. So, I think, did Conor.

Just before we reached home, he said, tentatively, "I'm going to say I caught that fish. OK?"

I said, "Conor, you absolutely caught that fish. That was what we call a 'long-distance release.'"

He liked that; things were going well. "And I'm going to say it was about this big," he added, holding his hands, I would guess, fifteen inches apart.

"It was all of that," I said. "Maybe more."

I could hardly believe my ears. I was encouraging this child, who already had a reputation for exaggeration, to lie. But of course, he knew that because of that very reputation, if he told the truth and said ten inches, his friends would assume he was exaggerating and mark it down to seven or eight, and that fish was much larger than any seven or eight inches! That would have been a real miscarriage of justice. Therefore, in order to arrive at the truth, Conor had to lie, and I had to help him. It was my responsibility as mentor and surrogate parent, same as that day it was my responsibility to feed those boys and keep them safe.

Later I realized that this was probably how it, the lying, all began: It was transmitted from father, or surrogate father, to son—not out of a need to impress, but out of love. It's the same impulse that leads us to overpraise our children's efforts in school or sports. "Good job!" we yell at a child's most feeble, clumsy efforts on the soccer field. And we mean it, and in our hearts it is the truth even if it isn't quite factual. And not only is it not harmful, or wrong, it is our duty as parents to tell these soothing lies. There's plenty of time later for them to learn life's cruel truths. Let someone else teach those.

After that I tended to be more philosophical about fish size; at least I tried to be. This past summer on the Kennebago River, my philosophy was put to the test. The Kennebago is fabled water; it's where rich folk used to fish when trains ran along its bank carrying sports to the camps on Kennebago Lake.

This past July Fourth the Kennebago was running high. Some of my usual places weren't fishable, but some places that were usually too shallow now held fish. In the first pool I caught two sixteen-inch salmon, not huge, but fresher and feistier than fall-run fish. As a bonus, one fish still carried a Black Ghost streamer in the corner of its mouth, tied with real jungle cock. I removed it, along with my own not-so-well-tied Gray Ghost, released the fish, and then promptly dropped and lost the nice Black Ghost. Oh well, it would take more than a lost fly to ruin this day.

I moved upriver. In the next fishable pool, I struck it rich. Standing on a rock in midstream, casting down and across braided water, I hooked fish after fish, including two eighteen-inchers, and lost another about that size. It almost never happens like that—in the middle of summer, midday, hot sun bearing down, the river theoretically too high, the fish insanely aggressive, chasing the fly, *any* fly. Eventually, after I'd hooked over a dozen, the action slowed. In the melee, I'd lost my landing net; who cared? I clambered off my rock, scrambled ashore, plowed back into the brush, and headed downriver to where I'd started, anticipating another bonanza, now that I had rested that pool.

Instead, I found another fisherman. I almost never encounter another fisherman at that pool. The water is not remote—nothing on that river is—but it's tucked away, unmarked and unmapped. But there he sat on the tailgate of his pickup, pulling off his waders. He had the same euphoric look on his face that I no doubt had on mine, until I saw him. Then all of a sudden I wasn't so happy.

The fisherman introduced himself—his name was Bill—and offered me a beer. I declined.

"How'd you do?" I asked unnecessarily. He'd clearly done quite well.

"Fabulous," he said. Between the previous evening and this morning, he had caught four fish over twenty inches.

Now I really didn't feel well. I've fished that pool for fifteen years and never caught even one twenty-inch fish. What a lousy fisherman I must be. "What'd you catch them on?" I asked. I wanted to know his secret. What had I been doing wrong?

"Streamers and weighted nymphs. They're holding right on the bottom," he said.

"What patterns?"

He named the common nymphs and streamers, including a Black Ghost.

That rang a bell. "I caught a fish this morning that had a Black Ghost in its mouth."

He smiled and shook his head. "I broke off a cawker last night." "Cawker," or corker, is local parlance for a really nice fish.

"I noticed the fly because it was so well tied."

"Thanks," he said.

"And it looked like real jungle cock."

He smiled, sipped his beer, and told me where he'd located a legal source of domestically raised jungle cock. No question, it was his fly all right, and his fish.

I shook my head. "That fish was twenty-two inches long," I said.

Bill wasn't the least fazed. "I knew he was a cawker."

I smiled; I had him now. He wasn't a better fisherman than I was; he was just a bigger liar. "Actually, that fish was sixteen inches long," I said a bit smugly.

Bill didn't bat an eye. Sixteen, twenty-two—what difference did it make? A cawker was a cawker. If I wanted to play games, that was my problem, his demeanor said. He was right, too. It was my problem. Hadn't I learned anything?

Actually, I had. It had finally sunk in: There are two types of numbers—one type we report to Fish and Wildlife, another type we use in conversation. They aren't the same units; they're as different as centimeters are from inches. In conversation, units of measure are figures of speech, metaphors. The answer to the question "How big was that fish?" is "How big does it need to be to gain your respect?" Not your respect for my prowess as a fisherman, but for the fish. In the right hands, it's not bragging to exaggerate fish size, and I had to admit, Bill's seemed like the right hands. He wasn't boasting; he was just happy, same as I ought to have been if I had any sense.

"On second thought," I said after a long silence, "maybe I will have that beer. If the offer still stands."

It did. We sat on the tailgate, making small talk, counting our blessings—a beautiful day, a gorgeous river full of fish, not much competition, a light breeze, not *too* many black flies. Before long, I was starting to feel pretty mellow myself. After all, it's not every day I take three twenty-one-inch fish from a single pool.

Slough Fever

SLOUGH:

    1. a place of deep mud and mire

    2. deep hopeless dejection or discouragement

    3. moral degradation

It's funny how fishing distorts the human mind and, for that matter, how fishing magazines distort the mind.

For example, my image of Dillon, Montana—an image derived entirely from fishing magazines—was of a picturesque village nestled snugly on the banks of the Beaverhead River. Downtown would consist of half a dozen fly-fishing shops, a restaurant or two, complete with pine-paneled walls lined with lunker browns, a gas station, and a couple of motels, both with fishing motifs. The parking places on Main Street would be occupied with pickup trucks trailering drift boats. Leaning against the gunwale of every other boat or so would be a lank, tanned guide in jeans and cowboy hat trading fishing yarns with fellow anglers.

The only accurate part of that image, I learned upon arrival, was the Beaverhead being the lifeblood of town. It is, not because of its fish, but because of its water. The Beaverhead irrigates the surrounding farms and ranches. Dillon is a farm town. There are towns like Dillon all over the Midwest. There are towns like Dillon in Maine: a downtown of decrepit brick buildings, surrounded by a periphery of fast-food joints, gas stations, convenience stores, and a freeway. The only sporting-goods store in downtown Dillon caters to bait fishermen. The only fly-fishing shop is tucked away on the edge of town. The Beaverhead River is even more elusive. I spent an entire morning searching for a suitable stretch to fish, but what I found was either unwadable, due to brushy banks and deep water, or posted. The posted signs were underlined with fresh strands of barbed wire.

Finally, about midday, I pulled into a trailer park that bordered a very fishable-looking stretch of river. What would I have to do, I asked the proprietress, to be allowed to fish the river from this property? She said I would have to rent trailer space for the night. It would cost me six dollars. "Cheaper than a spring creek," I said and was about to pull out the money, when she informed me that the trailer park owned only a few hundred feet of frontage. The rest of what I was looking at was posted. No one was allowed to fish there, ever. "But if you want good fishing," she quickly added, "you ought to try Poindexter Slough."

"You mean that little weed-choked stream I crossed on my way out here?" I hadn't come two thousand miles to fish something called a "slough."

"Poindexter Slough has some of the best fishing in Montana," she said defiantly.

I looked skeptically at her. Aside from being small, Poindexter Slough was close to town. It was too accessible. It even had a public parking lot. "Well, thank you very much for the information," I said, "but I have come to fish the Beaverhead."

The lady was insistent. Apparently I had offended her honor. She thrust out her chin and said, "Well, Jimmy Carter fished it when he came here."

I didn't see what that had to do with anything. He'd done a number of things I didn't approve of. Besides, Montana is a conservative state. They probably took Jimmy Carter to Poindexter Slough as punishment. But I did not want to argue politics. So I thanked the lady for her information, climbed back into my car, and drove slowly, despondently back up the road. It was early afternoon, and I hadn't wet a line.

As I was plotting a clandestine nighttime raid on the upper reaches of the Beaverhead, I remembered a conversation I'd had with my wife's cousin in Minnesota "I know *the* place to fish," he'd said. "It's called Poindexter Slough."

I didn't even listen to his directions. My wife's cousin is a wise, intelligent man, knowledgeable in almost every facet of life—business, science, literature—except fishing. The man knows nothing about fishing. Nothing. He has been once in his life, and yet here he was presuming to advise someone who had been researching this trip for months. "Thanks for the advice," I said, "but I believe I have the situation well in hand." Now, driving slowly back up the road to Dillon, I was beginning to wonder; I was starting to feel like the forces of destiny were ganging up on me.

I pulled into the Poindexter Slough parking lot beside a camper with Illinois plates and looked sullenly around at the other vehicles. There wasn't a Montana plate among them. Just as I suspected, Poindexter Slough was a tourist trap, but time was running out on this day. It was either Poindexter Slough or TV.

The Slough is a sinuous, slow-moving stream that flows into the Beaverhead. Due to its serpentine course, it is much longer than the meadow in which it lies. A single railroad bed parallels the meadow, providing access to the more remote (relatively speaking) reaches of the Slough. Wilderness fishing this is not.

Anglers are never out of sight of the interstate, and if Dillon had a skyline, you would be able to see it from Poindexter Slough. On the other hand, against a background of dry hills, the meadow is lush and green, and there is abundant wildlife along its edges— deer, ducks, wading birds. Beyond the road noises, there is an isolated, idyllic atmosphere.

The stream where I approached it was no more than twenty-five feet across. The water was exceedingly clear, with a bluish green tint that I attributed to the vegetation, which provided the only cover. There were no rocks, and the bottom was soft and sandy. Wading ruined the fishing yards downstream. I checked the water temperature. I didn't know at the time that Poindexter Slough was not a slough at all, but a spring creek, and I was shocked by the reading: sixty-two degrees. The air temperature was over eighty; the sun was bright and hot.

Still, I was not very hopeful as I followed a trail downstream, looking for signs of life, insects, rising fish, anything. Then I began to notice shadows scooting out from underneath the weeds ahead of me. Most were small, but some were not so small. I made a few futile casts, and each cast sent a few more fish scurrying for cover. It finally dawned on me that Poindexter Slough was full of fish. Every clump of weeds concealed fish. However, unless I changed my tactics, I was going to have to resign myself to fish watching.

I cut left out into the meadow, waded a few hundred yards through chest-high grass to another coil of stream. I crept toward the water, staying as low, moving as little as possible. There were fish rising in the stream. I moved back from the bank and began making long casts with a dry fly. For the next fifteen minutes I snagged weeds, grass, small limbs, snapped off flies, and spooked fish. By the time I had my technique under control, I had put the feeding fish down and was fishing blindly upstream to a bend with a deep undercut bank.

On my first cast a thick, speckled, reddish slab formed a crescent over my fly. The size of the fish—eighteen inches, I estimated—was too much of a shock for my system. The take had been too unexpected. I didn't set the hook so much as flinch in a rather dramatic manner, immediately snapping off the fly. "Damn!" The fish was not a trophy by Montana standards, but it was as good a fish as I had hooked all trip, and it hurt to lose it. On the other hand, any reservations I'd had about Poindexter Slough being worth the time and effort had been dispelled.

Around the next bend was a short, straight, deep pool, at the head of which four fish were feeding just below the surface. The most easily visible, the fish feeding in the main channel, was the largest of the four, a brown of about eighteen inches, the sibling of the fish I had just lost. The three feeding in the side chutes were in the twelve- to fourteen-inch range. This time there would be no mistakes. I crawled on hands and knees to within fifteen feet of the fish. He was in no more than three feet of water, holding about a foot below the surface, facing away from me, finning gently in the current. Occasionally he would tip his head to one side or the other, never moving more than a few inches for what must have been very small nymphs. I could see nothing in or on the water.

For the next hour I depleted my fly boxes—drys, wets, nymphs, bucktails, streamers, a Bett's Minnow, a Muddler Minnow—all to no avail. The best that could be said of my efforts was that at the end of the hour, all four fish were feeding as placidly as when I had arrived. This time I hadn't spooked them. On the other hand, I hadn't come close to catching them, not even a serious follow. Fly size, I was sure, was the problem. I had nothing smaller than a #16, and no nymphs smaller than a #12. There was no choice but to hurry back to the motel and tie more flies. I backed carefully away from the stream and hurried to my car.

When I arrived in the parking lot, I saw an elderly man carrying three slightly desiccated brown trout on a willow branch he had thrust through their gills and out their mouths. I quickly caught up to him. "What'd you catch those on?" I asked.

He had a glazed, feverish look in his eye. "On a little green fly," he said. "It was the only thing they would take."

"Could you be more specific?" I asked. "What was its name? What size was it?"

He shook his head in despair. "It didn't have a name. A friend gave it to me. It was the only one I had, and I lost it. I hung it on a branch. I tried wading out to it, but the bottom was too deep and soft."

"That's a shame," I said, "but can't you give me a better description?"

He shook his head but looked at me differently, with hope in his eyes. "You're a young man," he said. "I bet you're a stronger wader than I am. If you waded out and got it, then you could see exactly what it looked like. It was a hot fly for a while."

"Just tell me what it looked like. I'm going into town. I'll get some more. For both of us." I was starting to feel sorry for him. He seemed so forlorn. Also, he had a large scar on his neck. All the muscles had been removed from one side. I recognized the surgery. It was a radical neck dissection—a cancer operation.

"You can't buy this fly," he said. "It's not a traditional pattern." He held his fish up close to my face. "I caught several others besides these. I must have hooked a dozen."

"How far is it to your fly?" I asked, but what I really wanted to know was, what kind of cancer did he have? Was he cured? Was he on chemotherapy? What was his prognosis? If this was the last outing of a dying man, I wanted to know. I wanted to handle it with dignity.

"It wouldn't take you ten minutes to get down there," he said. "Fifteen at the most. I could take you right to the fly. I've got it marked."

Say he was telling the truth, with time out for wading, it would still take the better part of an hour. I looked at my watch, and at the sun falling like a rock toward the horizon. Then I took another look at his scar. It looked old and well healed. That surgery was a long time ago; that cancer was probably ancient history, and except for the scar, he looked pretty healthy. "Hell," I thought, "he's probably in better shape than I am." Then I looked at the fish and wondered how many more he would kill if I retrieved his fly. Didn't I have a responsibility to the resource?

"I'm sorry," I said. "It's getting late. If I go after your fly, then I won't have time to fish. I'm sorry."

He turned and walked sadly back to his camper, and I went to my car.

When my conscience finally caught up with me, I was back at the motel tying tiny nymphs. "My God," I thought, "what's happening to you? You used to be a decent guy, at least by your own standards."

I looked at myself in the mirror. I had a glazed, feverish look in my eyes. It was the same look that the old man had. It was identical. It was as if we had both been afflicted by the same febrile illness, and when I thought about it, I realized it was true, we had. We had contracted cases of an insect-borne disease, carried not by mosquitoes, but by caddis and mayflies. It was a form of mental illness transmitted from insect to man; the trout was the intermediate host. In our premorbid states probably neither of us would have acted as he did. The old man never would have asked a complete stranger to walk half a mile and wade a stream to retrieve a few grams of steel and feather. And I would not ordinarily have declined what might have been the last request of a dying man. I declared us both innocent by reason of insanity. Meanwhile, I had assembled sufficient microscopic nymphs to make another assault on the Slough and its selective trout.

I never caught that larger fish. Not that evening or the next morning. He was there on each occasion, feeding in the same station. The tiny nymphs at least made him nervous. His movements quickened, fins flared, but he never took. I hooked all three of the others, though. In the morning there was a breeze and the fish were downwind of me. No cast was required. I simply let the wind blow the leader down to the fish, let a light Cahill land, lift, dance on the water. They couldn't stand it, and each fish took the fly with the casualness of the genuinely deceived. Thank the wind for that. It gave life to my fly, and in return, of course, I released the fish. It was that sort of morning, acts of generosity begetting further acts of generosity. I felt clean and cured of last night's sickness. I hoped the old man would be in the parking lot and that he would ask a favor.

But he was not there, and I did not see his camper. I attempted to strike up conversations with several other fishermen, but they were in a hurry. They seemed tense and distracted, and looked at me with glazed, vacant stares. It was clear that the real focus of their attention lay somewhere behind me in the meadow.

Catch and Remember

ON A RECENT TRIP TO BELIZE, I LOST A GOOD BONEFISH. I LOST several, but this one was different. This was one I landed and a few hours later couldn't remember. Nothing, a total blank—and no fish, I'm now convinced, is more surely lost than those we catch and forget.

Not that we remember every fish forever. But I believe that if we see them clearly once, if we let their image sink in thoroughly, those fish will always be available, if not to our conscious mind, then to our unconscious. Like big fish everywhere, they'll come out at night into our dreams.

I know I caught that fish, because I distinctly remember the guide, Carlos, saying, "It is only 8:44, and already you 'ave caught three nice bones." Not 8:45, but 8:44, and I remember thinking, "Isn't it something that Carlos has a digital watch." I didn't have a digital watch.

I know that the fish had to have come from "nervous water," that quivering of the surface caused by fish cruising just beneath it, because the ones before and after had—the first and third fish, I remember clearly—and we hadn't moved far or changed our tactics. The plan had been to work the mangroves for tailing fish, but the tide was too low and the fish too far up in the mangroves, and the flats too soft to wade. So we lay along the edge like barracuda in ambush and watched in frustration at the tails shining in the morning sun.

The first fish came from a group that left the others and quartered left to right across our bow. "There," Carlos said. I saw them. The water was so smooth you could see wakes two hundred yards away. This can be a disadvantage. Too much time for the nerves to work, for fingers to fidget with fly line. I waited as long as I could before working out line, made one false cast, another, then let it go. The fly, a Horror, landed a few feet ahead of the apex of moving water. Carlos made a little noise in his throat that told me he was satisfied with the cast. We let the fly settle, then Carlos said, "Now strip. Strip. Strip. He sees it. He is following the fly. He is going to take the fly."

And so he did. I lifted the tip until I felt resistance, then delivered the loose coils of line, now suddenly violently alive, through the guides until the fish was on the reel. He bolted for the mangroves, and the reel made a sound like a mosquito very close to your ear.

Carlos was philosophical about our chances of catching that fish. "We don't often land the fish in here," he said. "The fun is in the hooking."

As I held the rod high to clear the smaller mangroves, Carlos began poling in the direction of my disappearing line, like a kid chasing a kite that has fallen in the woods. Except in this case, the woods were in the water. When we finally cleared the line, the fish was still there, resting. His second run took him away from the mangroves toward the turtle grass, a break for us. Carlos pushed us toward the open water. After two runs it was a tug-of-war, and soon the fish was landed and released. We agreed, we were lucky to have landed him. That was fish number one.

The third fish came from a flat flanked by a deep, sandy channel through which we'd been running full throttle until Carlos
spotted tailing fish and cut the engine. As we drifted to a stop, a
pelican swooped low over the flat, scattering the fish. We waited,
and soon the school reappeared in the form of nervous water far
away. Initially there was no pattern to the disturbance, just a dif-
fuse flickering of the surface. Then the fish organized and headed
straight toward us. "There are coming our way," Carlos said.
"They are going to come right to us."

I said nothing, but I didn't need that sort of comment upon
the obvious. The fish were charging us, and though I was not in
physical danger, there were mental hazards aplenty, all magnified
by Carlos's running commentary.

Three days earlier this would have been an automatic disaster,
but on day four, at least on this occasion, the timing was correct,
and the fly landed on target. Carlos made his little guttural noise
meaning "good cast," and simultaneously I felt the tug of the
fish—but he kept coming our way.

"He is staying with the school," Carlos said. "He is staying
with the others. I don't think he knows he is hooked."

So I told him. I stripped line until I felt resistance, then lifted
the rod tip, not hard, but firmly, then a second time. The fish
turned, and loose fly line danced around my feet, flirted with the
rod butt, but somehow found its way through the guides, then far
out onto the flats. There was a suspenseful moment of slack line,
but the fish was still on. He plunged into a deep, sandy, turquoise-
colored channel, and Carlos followed. "This fish is making me
work."

I heard an engine, looked up, and saw a tour boat bound for
the Mayan ruins at Altun Ha running full bore up the channel
toward my fly line and my fish. I applied pressure and horsed the
fish toward us, and Carlos leaned out and netted him just as the
boat sped by within thirty feet. Bad form, but we had our fish, a

nice three- to four-pound bonefish. In the sunlight, its scales shone like overlapping mirrors. Its back was barred with alternating shades of green. No wonder they're almost invisible in the water. Carlos released the fish, rinsed his hands, and that was when he said what time it was and what we'd caught—three nice bones—and I said, "Yes, we're off to a good start." So at that point, I must have known there'd been a third fish, but I was already too focused on what lay ahead to appreciate the fish we had already caught. I was looking past those fish to the future, because this was my final day. This was the day it would all come together; this was the day I would put up double figures.

On the day of my arrival, I'd overheard a conversation in the Belize City airport, two departing fishermen telling how in a week's time they'd taken two hundred bonefish. I think somewhere in the back of my mind I concluded that this was what bonefishing was all about—putting up big numbers that you could brag about in the airport, or not brag about but still feel smugly superior to those who caught fewer than you.

So in an effort to put up a big number, I posted another five. You might as well say four. That one fish was wasted on me. And during the remainder of the morning, in my haste to catch many fish, I managed to lose fish after fish due to carelessness, overconfidence, underconfidence, flukes of nature (a line snarling a mangrove that appeared out of nowhere), acts of God (a well-set hook simply falling out of a fish's mouth), but none of those fish were as permanently lost as the one I simply forgot. The others still live in my mind, but that one fish is gone for good, and that seems the least forgivable loss of all.

It wasn't until later that I discovered my loss, as if suddenly realizing my wallet was missing, or my watch. I was sitting at the bar, drinking a beer, gazing out at the lovely Caribbean, replaying the morning's events. It was like watching game films, except these could not be shut off. Suddenly I realized one fish was missing. The second fish of the morning. If Carlos had miscounted, I would've corrected him on the spot. He hadn't made a mistake; I had. We had caught three "nice bones" by 8:44; now one was gone. It was as if a piece of film had been excised and the cut ends spliced together. There was a depressing finality to it: I knew I would never see that fish again. And I haven't. No trick of memory has restored it to me. It was a total waste of a nice fish, and I ask myself, how could it have happened?

Looking back, I think what happened was, the second fish came too soon after the first. I hadn't fully recovered from the first fish. I was still absorbing the nervous water, the follow, the take, the fish blasting off into the mangroves, loose coils of fly line writhing like a berserk reptile. All that was still sinking in when the second fish came, and the mind was still in its refractory period.

So I've made a new rule never to catch more fish than I can assimilate. The actual number varies with species, but bonefish flood the senses with information, and few fish of any species are not worth remembering individually, at least for a while. The plan is, after each fish, to sit down and shut my eyes and let the fish's image sink in, to soak it up like the heat of the sun; to chat with the guide, to watch the wading birds in the mangroves and listen to the waves lap the side of the boat. And when I hear big talk in airports about one or two hundred fish in a week, to remind myself that big numbers don't have the staying power of a single medium-sized bonefish, and to reassure myself that if I fish attentively, no matter how many or how few fish I catch, I will have the stuff of which memories and dreams, real dreams, are made. Otherwise, why bother?

That same last morning I asked Carlos, "Do you ever dream of fish?"

"Sometimes," he said, without taking his eyes off the water or acting as if the question were the least bit strange.

My Time Among the Mainers

I NEVER REALIZED WHAT A STRANGE PEOPLE MAINERS ARE UNTIL I learned about their fishing superstitions. According to their beliefs, there are only three "game" fish in Maine: trout, salmon, and togue. All other fish, such as bass, perch, sunfish, and pickerel, are "rough" fish. Mainers believe that it is all right to catch "rough" fish for food just so long as you don't derive any pleasure from the actual catching.

The official canon for this ethic is encoded in L. L. Bean catalogs of the forties and fifties, before they became so secularized with bicycles, home furnishings, and other "consumer goods." Those early catalogs were dedicated to hunting and fishing and to the proposition that all fish were not created equal. Though it was never explicitly stated, it was clearly implied that the only fish in Maine were trout and salmon and that the only proper way to fish for them was with flies. As a youngster growing up in the South, it never crossed my mind that Maine had ordinary old southern fish like bass and pickerel. Perish the thought.

So in 1975, when I moved here, I taught myself to fly-fish for the practically sacred brook trout, and amazingly, I *caught some,* thereby discovering the first secret of brook trout's popularity: They're so easy to catch even a southerner can do it. They make everybody feel competent. The second secret of their popularity is taste; they're delicious. An aggressive delicacy—that's a death sentence for a fish. Most Mainers, I soon learned, regarded brookies primarily as "middlin fodder"—food! (Though I suppose that eating one is for them like taking communion.) No wonder the native fish are practically extinct, especially in Maine's fragile streams, most of which flow over granite bedrock, the stingiest possible source of nutrients. My hands aren't clean on that score either; I ate my share, but I was new and had no idea the damage one fisherman could inflict on a trout stream. I soon found out the hard way. Each year I fished harder and drove farther for fewer and smaller trout. And the price of gas was going up. It was time to explore other options.

Central Maine is dotted with lakes and ponds, which I had scrupulously ignored, because I had anointed myself not just a "trout fisherman," and not just a "fly fisherman," but a "dry-fly fisherman of flowages for native trout." No stocked fish for me, no streamers or wet flies either. I was the purest of the pure. It was clearly time to reassess my fishing priorities. What about these abundant stillwaters that virtually surrounded me? What about— God forbid!—bass?

Even though a southerner, I was a saltwater fisherman; I knew nothing about freshwater fishing. So I bought a few books, picked up some popping bugs, and one sunny, still, late September afternoon in 1980, I decided to go, not fishing, but canoeing (an important distinction) on nearby North Pond with my nonfishing wife and five-year-old nonfishing son. I took my fly rod almost as an afterthought, the way the old-timers would take a sidearm into the woods for self-defense.

The pond was calm and empty. Not a single other boat spoiled the solitude. From the shore came the sad sounds of hammering;

camps were being closed for the winter. The sounds lent a poignancy to the warmth of the sun. (Winter always hangs like a sword over Maine summers, though lately a warming trend has dulled its edge.) We paddled slowly up the pond; my son's hand dangled lazily overboard. An osprey circled overhead. The pond was a portrait of tranquility. We meandered onward. Then, several hundred feet ahead, there was a faint, barely perceptible distur-bance of the surface. Circles dotted the water as if from a light rain, but there wasn't a cloud in the sky. It appeared that a pod of fish was feeding. The riseforms were so small and subtle—not a genuine swirl among them—I was certain it was perch or sunfish causing the disturbance.

"I'll make a cast anyway," I said without much enthusiasm. I worked out fly line and made a perfunctory cast with a small white popper toward the nearest dimple. For a few moments nothing happened, and then a gaping mouth, a maw, rose slowly beneath my tiny popper. Then, like a football thrown through a plate glass window, an enormous smallmouth shattered the sur-face, snatched my popper, rose several feet into the air, gave a vio-lent shake, and sent my popping bug flying back at me. The fish fell back into the water, and everything was calm once more. Hammering from the nearby camps continued just as if nothing out of the ordinary had happened, just another tranquil afternoon on North Pond, but I knew that my fishing life would never be the same.

That winter I bought more books on bass fishing, survey maps of Central Maine ponds, and in the spring I went exploring with my fly rod. Virtually every rocky shoreline held smallmouth. Usu-ally the fish were feisty and aggressive; they assaulted the popper, then catapulted into the air. Other times they were remarkably troutlike. More than once I found them sipping mayflies from the surface as daintily as any brookie. Once I found a smallmouth holding beneath a log, feeding on mayfly duns carried by a light breeze. The fish refused to take a popper; so, not having any duns on hand, I switched to a hare's ear nymph, and the fish took on the first cast. I was proud of us both, me for figuring out the problem, the fish for its troutlike selectivity. (Nowadays I would never "compliment" a bass by calling it troutlike; now it would be the other way around.)

It was when I tried to spread the good news about bass to my trout-fishing friends that I first encountered the snooty New England attitude toward nonsalmonids. One local outdoor writer even said in print that he would rather mow his lawn than fish for bass—this from a man who *trolls* for salmon. I love salmon, but trolling for anything is more boring, and no more sporting, than gill netting. Or, for that matter, mowing the lawn.

Once, assuming this New England attitude was correctable, I took a trout-fishing friend of mine, Dan, bass fishing on Parker Pond. Parker is the most pristine and beautiful of all the local ponds, dotted with small, forested islands; there are miles of rocky shoreline, wonderful habitat for smallmouth bass. There's also a put-and-take salmon fishery. Immediately after ice-out there's a trolling frenzy, same as on the other salmon ponds, but by late May the trollers have moved north, and in those days Parker would be pretty much deserted.

The evening Dan went was calm and overcast, and we caught over a dozen nice fish. He hooked and lost several before overcoming his trout-taught reluctance to *set* the hook. Then he landed a respectable specimen, fifteen inches, a pound and a half. The fish pulled harder than a trout and jumped several times, which a brook trout almost never does. Finally, Dan lipped the fish and let him go. "They are right spunky," he allowed condescendingly. That was the best he could do; yet he gets ecstatic over eight-inch brook trout. I think the problem is that Mainers see brook trout as more than a mere fish. Brookies evidently symbolize primitive New England, the wilderness that once was

Maine, and they apparently look at bass the same way they look at other out-of-staters: If they aren't native, they can't be worth much. It's not just bass, either. Another fishing acquaintance of mine invariably refers to brown trout, which are slowly taking over brook trout waters, as "*German* browns," his tone of voice and facial expression implying "foreign, therefore inferior." Never mind that brown trout are hardier and more selective than brookies, and they jump. They're also real trout, *Salmo trutta,* not char, like the *Salvelinus fontinalis.* None of which makes a particle of difference to native Mainers, who take great pride in their prejudices.

After my experience with Dan, I got out of the missionary business and quit proselytizing on behalf of a fish that shouldn't need it. Either you see it or you don't. If you don't, it's your loss. As for me, I went bass fishing, which in those days I had virtually to myself. One problem with smallmouth bass, I soon learned, was that when the water warms and spawning is over, they go deep and become very difficult to catch with poppers. I'm addicted to the surface action, the splashy strike, or the quieter, swirling take: dorsal fin, broad, dark back, solid hookup, the heaviness of a good fish. Even a missed fish releases adrenaline, sometimes more than one that's hooked, because the mystery of size remains. So rather than pursue midsummer smallmouths deep, I switched species and locales: from rocky shorelines to lily pads and shallow coves; from smallmouth to largemouth.

There's no record of exactly when largemouth were introduced to Maine, but it was after smallmouth. Now they're everywhere. Practically every pond in Central Maine holds bass of both species; I'm surrounded by bass. The beauty of largemouth is, they offer surface action all summer long, when tender brook trout are sulking in spring holes and smallmouth are hard to find. Often the largemouth feed on insects, damselflies, and caddis. On summer evenings local ponds are alive with rising bass. It isn't *like* dry-fly fishing; it *is* dry-fly fishing, except the fish are larger than brook trout, take more violently, and fight harder.

Fifteen years later, bass are no longer a secret. Now they are the most sought-after fish in Maine, even by Mainers, whose bass-fishing role models (thanks to cable TV) are people such as Hank Parker, Jimmy Houston, and Roland Martin—southerners, in other words. As a transplanted southerner myself, I can't help but be amused. Of course, many trout fishermen still make fun of bass fishermen because they fish from overpowered candy-colored boats, wear jumpsuits covered with decals, and use terms like "hawg" and "pig'n jig." The irony is that in Maine, bass fishermen have done a better job taking care of bass than trout fishermen have of trout. Bass fishermen have demanded—and gotten—tighter, not looser, regulations. Most Maine trout fishermen just want more trout and don't much care where they come from. Hatchery or natural—all roads lead to the frying pan.

As an indication of its popularity, bass fishing has finally infiltrated L. L. Bean, Maine's bastion of hunting and fishing, its arbiter of outdoor taste. Bean's cathedral-like retail store in Freeport—a celebration of post-and-beam architecture, with richly burnished, laminated hardwood arches and trusses, where antique fishing tackle and sepia-tinted photos of the old days are displayed like religious relics—now carries bass-fishing gear. Up to a point. They have a full collection of bass flies, lovely deer-hair frogs with jointed legs and doll's eyes, ornately decorated Dahlberg Divers, and gorgeous blue damselflies. They also carry a small but adequate supply of spinning tackle—rods, reels, a few soft plastic lures, along with crankbaits, spinners, and spoons—but they do not carry, as far as one can tell from looking, a single bait-casting rod or flipping stick, the favorite weapons of the serious bass angler.

This glaring deficiency seemed so odd to me that on a recent visit I mentioned it to the salesperson, a friendly young woman who corrected me and said that, in fact, Bean's did carry bait-casting tackle.

I said, "Oh, I didn't see any. I saw lots of spinning rods, but no bait casting."

"They may not be on display," she said. "But I can find them if you want. I think they may be under the counter or out back."

"No, no," I quickly said. "That's OK, I'll take your word for it. I was just curious. That's all."

I didn't like the sound of "under the counter," and I didn't like how the saleslady looked at me. I suddenly felt like a teenager trying to buy prophylactics from the local pharmacist. As I was backing out of her department, I tried to explain to the woman that I was a fly fisherman myself, that, although I did fish for bass, I would never actually use a bait-casting rod (I wouldn't) or go speeding around in one of those tacky boats, and I'd never wear a jumpsuit (God!). I was only asking for research purposes, and blah blah blah, until finally I was out of her department, back among my own kind in the fly-fishing section. But it was a close call.

An addendum: *Mirabile dictu,* my trout-fishing friend, Dan, recently bought some bass flies, and used them. His daughter's boyfriend, a fly fisherman, a westerner, accomplished in one visit what I hadn't been able to do in fifteen years of preaching and cajoling. He convinced Dan it wasn't just OK to fish for bass; it could actually be fun (evidently they caught a couple of really nice smallmouth), and it didn't mean you were a bad person if you enjoyed it. Mother Teresa could not have been more pleased with his conversion.

Turning Forty Near the Fork

ON THE EVE OF MY FORTIETH BIRTHDAY I MADE A PILGRIMAGE TO the so-called fly-fishing Mecca of America, the Henry's Fork of the Snake. I was sorely disappointed. The river was too placid, too sullen, and too parsimonious for my tastes.

A line of elderly men in elaborate fly-fishing outfits stood as motionless as herons along the riverbank. The river and those men seemed ideally suited for each other. The river and I were not.

Without making a single cast, I got back in the car and drove to the Osborne Bridge. I hiked through a meadow to a stretch of riffles where I could actually hear and see a current. So what if it wasn't "big fish" water? At least it wasn't a lake. It was alive!

I quickly caught two smallish rainbows, about ten inches— legal there—and creeled them both. It wasn't meant as a sacrament or ritual or any of that religious business—this was a magazine writer's notion of Mecca, not mine. Those two fish were food, maybe a quick "take that!" to the river, and nothing more. I was out of sorts and had been for a while, and it wasn't nice of me to take it out on those fish—if that's what I was doing—but by the time I got around to analyzing it, it was too late for them anyway. They were on ice, and I was hell-bent for the Warm River. Besides, fly fishing, for all its poetic aspects, is a blood sport. Fish do die, and I doubt they care what kind of mood we're in when we kill them, or what sort of significance we attach to the act. Sacrament or anger—it's all the same to them.

The Warm River, I had read, was like a miniature Henry's Fork except the current was heavier and the fish lighter. It was a freestone river, not technical like the Fork. I took a circuitous route through the Targhee National Forest; OK, I was lost, and it was slow going anyway over a dusty gravel road, where free-range cattle roamed fearlessly. It was almost sundown when I found the river.

It turned out that the Warm River is a) not warm, and b) not really even a river for much of its length, just a little stream. Then abruptly, dramatically, it is joined by Warm River Spring, an icy torrent that gushes and spews out of a rock wall. Then it's a full-fledged river with riffles, pools, glides, and rapids tumbling steeply through a lush, green valley, a valley with no road running beside it and no old men lining its banks like wading birds.

There was one fisherman in the uppermost pool, next to the parking lot. His was the only car, and there was no indication he was staying, no tent or camper. That meant in the morning I would have that river to myself. Hallelujah. But first I had to get through the night.

As a rule I don't camp. To me the paraphernalia of camping— tents, stoves, pegs—are the enemy of fishing. I own a sleeping bag, and in an emergency, if there's no motel in easy driving range of my intended river, I'll sleep in the back of the car, in this case, my wife's Subaru wagon. I'm even capable of preparing a small meal. I'd brought a few rudimentary utensils, plus flour, cooking oil, coffee, potatoes, a bottle of wine, and I still had my two fish. (I've since invested in a Sterno cook "stove" that will actually fold up and fit inside a fishing vest and is perfectly satisfactory for warming coffee water or a can of beans, though not at the same time.)

But in the Targhee, campfires are permitted, and I soon located a firepit not far from the river in a semiarid clearing of sage and scrub pine, surrounded by taller pines. I parked the car, collected firewood, and by dusk I had a roaring blaze and soon a bed of coals. I fried my fish, boiled potatoes, and drank the bottle of wine, slowly savoring my surroundings and the solitude, which, when the other fisherman left, was complete.

I needed and enjoyed that solitude. It had been a rough decade, a decade of losses, mostly domestic, with a few more to come—the sorts of things, which in the absence of real tragedy, a war for example, will do quite nicely. Then the alcohol kicked in. Good stuff, alcohol, the best anesthetic money can buy without a prescription. In moderation, of course. (My father's motto, "Everything in moderation." It should've been his epitaph.)

The wine made it possible to enjoy the evening: the campfire, the anticipation of the river, and soon, the two coyotes that called back and forth across the clearing. I tried to make it a trio, but even inebriated, I couldn't carry a tune or even howl convincingly. The coyotes certainly weren't fooled or, as best I could tell, amused. So screw the coyotes, if they couldn't take a joke. It was my birthday; if I felt like howling, I would—and did. I had a hell of a time, my best birthday in at least a decade.

In the morning, possessed by a sort of giddy euphoria that sleep deprivation can produce, I hit the river on a dead run, before sunup and before any other fishermen, of which there were none anyway. I fished that river to the point of exhaustion, and then I fished some more. I caught rainbow after rainbow on nothing more sophisticated than Royal Wulffs and Hoppers. It was not a technical river, and the fish weren't large, but the pleasure of the day was immense, immeasurable, and though I didn't know it then, it would last a long time and, somehow, console me when nothing else could.

The whole valley was mine. One side was steep and wooded, the other, where I fished, meadowlike, until away from the river it rose abruptly in rocks and sage. As the day wore on and the sun began to sink, I contracted a full-blown case of Rapture of the River: a compelling need to know what was around the next bend. I had to know. I couldn't bring myself to turn back. Every bend seemed more promising, more beautiful and pristine than the next. Surely the fish would be larger farther downriver, and sometimes they actually were. And the fever grew worse and worse toward evening. I couldn't turn around, and my fishing grew more and more frantic. Cast, mend, and set the hook, or change the fly, release the fish, but whatever you do, don't stop moving. I tripped and stumbled, tore shirt and boots, lost my net and forceps, but I found something far more important—I discovered that, all evidence to the contrary notwithstanding, I still had the capacity for happiness, even joy. Yes, there was more pain ahead, probably worse pain, but even that was preferable to the state of suspended animation I had been living in.

And I knew that whatever happened, however things worked out, this river or others like it would be waiting for me. No matter what, the rivers would still love me. At least it felt like love, and that was good enough for me.

Fluency

FLUENCE:

   1. a stream

   2. an easy flow of words

Fish, water, words. Fish make us garrulous. Fish incite us to verbiage—the evidence is all around us, fishing books proliferating like mayflies. Some of us even dream in fish; fish are the coin of the realm, the currency of our subconscious minds.

For years spring creeks were a recurring theme of my dream life, spring creeks and the contrast between their rich, lush, fertile waters and the rest of the world, which by comparison was a virtual desert.

In one dream I was flying over an actual desert. Below me, drawn on the earth, was a perfect circle divided into two parts, one green, one beige, as if half the field had been irrigated, the other half left to fend for itself. Or like a pie chart, a personal inventory of a self divided. Later, the dream took a slightly different shape. This time the desert was punctuated by potholes, which, on closer examination, were deep, fecund ponds that, lo and behold, held fish, four- to five-pound rainbow trout. Not only that, but the ponds were connected underground; the trout could circulate among the ponds. Frantically—there was an urgency to the dream—I began digging up the earth between the ponds by hand. It was like a surgical procedure, removing a crust or scab to reveal healthy, rich subterranean waters.

The dream was sneakily powerful; I awakened in a state of shock. This earth-moving operation of my dream was more than simple excavation or an overly ambitious fishing expedition. It was soul searching and thirst quenching all at once, because it suggested a connection between aridity and the inaccessibility of language, and hinted at a missing link between thought and language, a liquid, fertile, fish-filled world beneath a parched surface.

My background is in medicine, but I was a fisherman long before I was a doctor—and long after. My troubled relationship with medicine gave rise to all sorts of escapist fantasies and dreams, even after the escape physically had been made. Usually I would be in a hospital about to make rounds, or about to begin a new rotation, or sometimes actually treating a patient, but always I would be unlicensed, an impostor, about to be found out and banished (yippee!) from medicine. Or occasionally I would be about to leave on my own, but I was never quite able to make that break until one night a river literally came to my rescue.

This time I wasn't inside a hospital, but outside, standing on the hospital steps. Behind me the building loomed large and alabaster white, modern and sterile. Before me swirled a river, its waters actually lapping the marble staircase. The contrast could not have been more stark: the sterile, impersonal monolith behind me versus the swirling, fertile, fish-laden waters at my feet. This was the moment I'd been waiting for, and these were the waters I'd been craving. This was the night I was definitely taking my leave of medicine. The only problem was that the river, actually a large spring creek, surrounded the hospital, which rose like Atlantis from its waters. I couldn't drive, and I didn't have a boat.

As I stood there befuddled, a drift boat floated by carrying two fly fishermen and a guide, and somehow I realized I was in Montana, where, for a long time, like most fly fishermen, I'd longed to be. This was the night all the pieces of my various long-ings and yearnings came together. Briefly I considered trying to hitch a ride, but even in the happiest of dreams, guides are guides, surly and irascible, and very territorial. This one didn't seem to like how I looked at his boat. In fact, he seemed to resent my very presence, as if perhaps I would spook *his* fish. So I waited until he'd passed. Then, tired of waiting—I'd been waiting for ages—and without even removing my hospital whites, I entered the water fully dressed.

The water was comfortably warm (but somehow still suitable for trout). I treaded water to get my bearings. Then I started swimming downstream around a bend and toward a distant curve. Somehow I knew exactly where I was going. I was going home. And I knew what I was going to do when I got there. I was going to fish and I was going to write. In me the two were inextricably connected. The missing link all along was simply my reluctance to enter the water, to swim, to fish, and to live.

A Big Afternoon on
Little Cayman

LIFE AT LITTLE CAYMAN ISLAND'S SOUTHERN CROSS CLUB IS SO placid that some people are actually bothered by the surf. One disgruntled fellow complained over breakfast that the noise of the waves kept him awake.

I was incredulous. "Some people play recordings of that sound to help them sleep."

"I'm used to the quiet," he said.

"I thought you were from New Jersey."

He corrected me. "I'm from the *mountains* of New Jersey."

That was a new one. I started to tell him I was from the desert of Maine—there actually is one, though nobody lives there—but the tranquil atmosphere simply wasn't conducive to bickering.

Later that morning, my son Preston and I took the dive boat to Little Cayman's famous North Wall. From two thousand feet above the ocean floor, looking down was like gazing up at the evening sky: Fish hung in the water like hawks or eagles riding thermals, and beyond the last visible fish the water darkened to royal blue, then turned black as ink or outer space. Too spooky for me, and we weren't scuba diving, we were snorkeling. So we headed inshore, where just a few yards on the wall's other side, the water was barely three fathoms deep and was dotted with coral, dappled with sunlight. This place seemed friendly and benign; sea fans beckoned us like welcoming hands. Foolish-looking parrot fish nibbled coral and ignored us. It was intriguing that two such contrasting worlds existed in such close proximity. Problem was, I didn't come to Little Cayman for intrigue; I came to fish. The snorkeling was for Preston.

In those days, Little Cayman claimed to offer the "world's best bonefishing." The bonefishing has since been downgraded to "world class," but even that's debatable. The "world's most laid-back bonefishing" would be more like it.

Basically, either you made blind casts to "muds" or you and your guide meandered along the coral beach looking for fish tailing in the turtle grass. My guide, William, was a Montanan of the lackadaisical, New West persuasion. He wore shorts, no shoes, no shirt, and sported a "world class" tan. It may even have been the "world's best" tan. He carried his fly-fishing tools—for the most part ornamental—around his neck on a rubber lanyard that he rotated periodically least his tan be spoiled by the pale outline of a pair of forceps stenciled onto his chest.

Strolling along the rocky shore, we saw an occasional uncooperative bonefish and very occasional uncooperative permit (the only kind of permit that exist, in my experience). "We probably ought to advertise the permit fishing more," the guide said.

I thought, "You probably ought to advertise the walking," but I didn't say anything. For what I was paying, I wasn't willing to admit I wasn't having fun. I could hear my financial clock ticking, which, when you think about it, defeats the purpose of paradise, destroys the illusion that under the right circumstances you could actually live here. Fact was, paradise came at a very high price: over ten dollars an hour per person, day and night. We couldn't afford a whole week; for me, every moment was precious. The meter was running.

William, on the other hand, seemed to have all the time in the world. He was on winter leave from the Montana fishing lodge where he worked summers. Clearly, this was an off-season gig for him, and his heart wasn't in it. So on our third and final day, I gave him the afternoon off; I guess you could say I fired him. He didn't seem to mind.

After lunch I went alone to Owen Island, a dot of sand and scrub within Little Cayman's lagoon, sort of an island within an atoll. Owen is flanked on one side by hard white sand, as flat as a tabletop, covered by a thin layer of water as transparent as Plexiglas. On my first day I'd seen a large school of bonefish feeding on that flat, as easily visible as a museum exhibit. Someone was fishing for them, but William said there was no use wasting time on those fish. They'd been cast to so often they were virtually uncatchable, which, from my experience, didn't distinguish them from any other fish in that area.

The fish were already feeding on the flat when I arrived, but they were so exposed that even the shadow of a frigate bird scattered them in all directions. But soon, I noticed, the school reformed and resumed feeding. Not only that, there was a pattern to their movement. They weren't grazing randomly; they were ever so slowly circling the flat clockwise. A slight breeze rippled the water and offered a little cover, but it also meant I would have to position myself upwind.

As the fish were making a downwind tack, I crept out and kneeled in the water. And waited. The water was so shallow and the sun so bright that the fish stood out like lead ingots against the sand, even from a hundred yards away. Their slow, steady migration was easy to follow. Soon the school reached the far end of the small flat and turned toward me. I slouched lower but kept the waterline below my chest so the drumbeat of my heart wouldn't spook the fish. When the school's leading edge was in range, I made a single false cast. The fly line's shadow sliced the school of fish as cleanly as a sharp knife. By the time the school reassembled and settled down, it was out of casting range. There was nothing to do but wait, but waiting was a pleasure: puffy clouds, blue sky, warm sun, light breeze, visible feeding bonefish, and the anticipation of their return.

Also, on the flats I felt safe. I don't always have to play predator—I can soak up esthetics as well as the next person—but I certainly don't like playing prey, or potential prey. Fact was, floating facedown atop a two-thousand-foot column of water beside the Wall with my tender parts exposed, I felt afraid. I know sharks and barracuda almost never attack divers, but they could. They could shred you in seconds. Bonefish may break your heart, but at least they don't bite. I like that in a fish. I'm not seeking adventure or danger in my fishing; ordinary day-to-day life in America—even in Maine—offers more than enough danger for me.

The next time the fish came my way, I let them get within point-blank range before I cast, so close that even kneeling, I had to hunker until I was almost sitting in the water in order not to spook them with my shadow, so close that I was looking more sideways than down. I could see their eyes, mouths, and individual scales. My cast was nothing more than a flip of the leader and a couple feet of fly line. A twitch of my arm, plink of fly near the perimeter of the school. No going over the top of them this time. I clearly saw the fish that took my fly. He casually moved a few feet from the school, sucked my Crazy Charlie, and swam leisurely away. Not wishing to spook the fish, I didn't bother setting the hook. I merely let the line tighten, and then, as casually as the fish took the fly, he released it. He didn't spit it out; the fly simply fell from his mouth like a particle of food. If he felt the hook, it must have registered only as "inedible," not "danger." He never spooked, but he was gone nonetheless.

Slowly the school meandered over the flat, until once again an edge was within fifteen or twenty feet of me, about twice the length of my leader. Another flip cast brought another take at point-blank range. This time I lifted the rod tip and ever so gently set the hook. The fish bolted from the school, darted straight toward the turtle grass and the darker, deeper water. I didn't stand up, and the other fish never spooked. There was a brief disturbance in the vicinity of the hooked fish, a flurry of motion as the rest of the school closed ranks and resumed feeding, evidently assuming that whatever urgent business had summoned their colleague to the turtle grass was no threat to them.

The hooked fish somehow managed to locate and wrap the only mangrove shoot on the entire flat. If I had been standing, I could easily have lifted the line over the little plant, but from my knees, the angle of the line favored the fish. That's all a bonefish needs, one little slip. They're quick to take advantage, and before I even realized my line was wrapped, the fish was gone.

By now the sun was getting low. That meant no more fussing around, no more squandering hooked fish in order to preserve the tranquility of the school. Time to commit to actually catching one.

As the light faded, the school seemed to move more slowly than ever. It oozed over the flat like an amoeba, pseudopods of fish extending first in one direction, then another, but the organism as a whole moved steadily over the sand. Finally the fish found their way back to me. I had the hooking business down to a science: flip the wrist, raise the rod tip, feel the resistance. Except this time when the fish took, I jumped to my feet and raced across the flat with the rod held high overhead. The flat around my feet exploded as fish raced off in all directions spraying water everywhere, as if the flat were being raked by machine gun fire.

My fish's first run took it far out into the turtle grass. The reel's whine made the fish's speed audible. I stood on the edge of the hard sand flat, rod held high like an antenna, which in a sense it was. Its pulsations carried the low-pitched, tactile throbs. The high-pitched notes came through the line and out the reel. (Fly rods and reels are by far the best tackle for transmitting signals from fish; they're much better listening devices than spinning or bait gear. And reel makers should pay more attention to the musical quality of their instruments. They're creating the soundtrack to our memories.)

Strictly speaking, I never landed my fish. I didn't "bring him to hand," but in my opinion he was "in hand" the whole time. And "in ears" and "in eyes." He filled the senses; he satisfied.

That evening I sought out my erstwhile guide, William, not to gloat—OK, maybe to gloat a little—but as a public service, for future reference, to let him know that those fish were not totally untouchable. I told him the truth. "I didn't land a single fish, but I hooked three and had a great afternoon." I didn't mention that I had traumatized the whole school by leaping up like the creature from the Black Lagoon and charging across the flat, stampeding the fish. If William's next client had trouble stalking those fish, so much the better for my reputation. "Yep," I could picture William saying in his slow western drawl, "only one man's been able to hook those fish. And we never really got to know him . . ." At which point the strains of the *William Tell* Overture would rise in the background. Of such stuff fishing legends are born. Or maybe not.

When I found William, he was playing bridge with the other guides. He looked up when I approached, and when I told him about my afternoon, he raised his eyebrows—*both* eyebrows—so I knew he was impressed. He even gave an approving little nod of his head. Then, as if to say I wasn't the only one with talent, he told me that the very same afternoon, he had bid and made six no trump, doubled and redoubled. It was the talk of the island.

Swimming the Selway

I DO LOVE TROUT, BUT I WOULD NOT WANT TO DIE FOR ONE. Only once have I come close, and even now I am not sure how close I actually came.

It was the summer of '82, and my wife had just given birth to our second consecutive nonfisherman. This called for a trip to Minnesota to visit the in-laws. It seemed to me the perfect time to fish. "Do you realize," I said, "that it is less than a day's drive from your parents' place to the Montana border?" I said it would be a shame to drive all that way from Maine and not go to Montana. It would be like false labor. She could relate to that.

Besides, this was her moment, not mine. At a time like this, who needed a husband lurking around in the background bragging about how he helped with the breathing. The least I could do was get out of the way. The way I saw it, I did Lamaze; I paid my dues. Now it was time to fish. And that was what I did. After thirty-six hours in Fergus Falls—that's a long time in Fergus Falls—I bolted for I-94, Fargo, and points west.

If you love the West but live in the East, there is a fever that overtakes you as you leave deciduous trees, as the land dries and rises toward the Rockies. If you fly-fish, the fever is even worse, and fishing does not slake it. If anything, it aggravates it. If you fish alone, you are particularly vulnerable to a sort of agitated euphoria, wherein nothing matters but the fishing; nothing else exists. Drive, fish, eat, sleep, eat, fish, drive, sleep—the life cycle of the traveling fly fisherman. If you're not careful, it can be as ephemeral as a mayfly's.

By the time I arrived at the Selway-Bitterroot Wilderness Area, I had been on the road a week. Time was running out, and I was in a hurry. So much water; so little time. After hastily signing in at the ranger station, I skidded to a halt in the parking lot, donned fishing gear, and hurried upriver. How far I get up any river is a function of how badly I want to escape parking lots and people, on the one hand, and the appeal of the river, its drawing power, on the other.

I did not get very far up the Selway. There were no other fishermen, and the Caribbean clarity of the river proved too alluring. For someone accustomed to fishing in iced tea, the clarity of the Selway was stunning—and deceptive. The river was braided where I began fishing. I took a medium-sized cutthroat of tropical coloration from the closest run, then looked across the river for better water. I found an enticing stretch on the other side, a lovely deep run against the bank. To reach it, I had to wade a narrow tongue of water. I was wearing hip boots, not waders, but the water did not appear to be more than two feet deep. I could count the pebbles on the bottom, and before I took my first step, I considered that run crossed and was looking ahead to the next and beyond that to the dark chute beside the far bank, where there was no road and God only knew how many trout.

My first step never touched bottom. It hasn't to this day. The current hit me low, like a blindside block at the knees, knocked me off my feet, and carried me quickly downriver into deep water. Before I had gone a hundred feet, before fear had even registered, I hit a sweeper, a dead softwood stretched like a loving arm into the river. I must have been rotating as I bobbed downstream, because I caught the tree in the right ribs. As one indication of current speed, I couldn't sleep on that side for weeks, but the pain felt wonderful at the time. I embraced the tree with all four extremities like a possum, then slowly, carefully pulled myself on top. My lower half was still submerged, my legs locked around the tree, but for the moment I was safe. I started tossing gear onto the bank, less than twenty feet away. First the rod, then net, vest, hat, glasses. Then I shinnied, crawled, clambered to shore. I pulled off and drained my boots and stretched out in the sun. For the first time in a week, I didn't feel like fishing.

What I did not know at the time was that almost at the exact moment I was lying there beside the Selway, my wife was reporting me missing to authorities in three states. Not only that, she contacted friends in Arizona, Wyoming, and Seattle to see if they had heard from me. She called relatives in Virginia. She even had VISA tracking my trail of credit card receipts. Apparently there had been some confusion about my itinerary, understandable since I did not have an itinerary. And there was a question of a missing phone call. In fact, I had been quite good about checking in, very good, but the public phone at the West Fork Lodge in Darby, Montana, had been out of order when I had stayed there a couple of days before. I had tried everything. I shook it, rattled it, kicked it. Nothing worked. Who could say where the next public phone was? Hamilton? Missoula? Spokane? What was I supposed to do, spend all day looking for a phone? No, I was supposed to fish the West Fork of the Bitterroot, and that was what I did. I hadn't promised a phone call that day, anyway. She had simply been expecting one because of the timing of earlier calls. So her telepathy was correct as far as it went; it just hadn't gone far enough. Defective telepathy, malfunctioning phones—the deck was stacked against me.

It would make a nice story to say that, chastened by my drenching, suddenly reminded of my mortality, I hurried back to Minnesota to attend to my family responsibilities. But this is nonfiction, and what actually happened was, I sat up and tallied my losses. The camera was ruined, and a roll of film. I could replace the camera, but it hurt to lose that roll of film. There were some good fish on that roll, and losing it was like losing all of them at once. The cork grip of my rod was scarred with deep teeth marks from when I had needed both hands to hold on to the tree, but the reel was fine. It had landed softly and had not even been knocked out of round. My flies were in little swimming pools, but they would dry, as would the boots. My ribs were bruised, and I could not take a deep breath. So? I would take more frequent, shallower ones. All in all, I decided, things could have been worse.

To see just how much worse things could have been, to see what might have happened without the tree, I walked downstream. The tail of the pool shoaled up nicely to a depth of two feet or less. Probably I could have climbed out there, even without the tree. Surely I could have. Below the pool, the different threads of current re-formed into a single strand of heavy water. Then there was a waterfall, but why dwell on that? I would have been out long before that.

Having settled that issue, I returned to the car, changed clothes, and headed off to my next destination. I fished a few more uneventful days before heading back to Fergus Falls. When I arrived at my in-laws', right on time on the Sunday afternoon I had said I would be back, my wife was not around. She was at a hypnotist's trying to recall, under hypnosis, the exact details of our last conversation. Where was it I had said I was going? Which direction? I was amazed. "A hypnotist!?" I said. "On a Sunday afternoon? I had no idea this town offered such amenities. I underestimated it." I still wasn't taking the missing part very seriously. It still hadn't quite sunk in just how many people she had contacted, or how she had portrayed this incident, or how it might have been perceived by certain relatives in Virginia who had a distorted, not necessarily favorable image of, in no particular order, fly fishing, Montana, and me.

When my wife returned from the hypnotist—no luck—we had a spirited debate on the appropriateness of her behavior versus how hard I should have tried to find a working telephone. Between rounds, we notified the various authorities, friends, and family members of my miraculous reappearance. No one living west of the Mississippi seemed seriously concerned. Certain members of the Virginia wing of the family were moderately hysterical; they still are, and to this day will bring the incident up as an example of my irresponsibility. I reject this argument in its entirety. These people do not fish. *Res ipsa loquitur.*

My wife and I never did settle the argument. It went on intermittently for months like an underground fire we could never completely extinguish. Ultimately, inevitably, the argument outlasted the marriage.

At no time during our discussions did I mention my brief unscheduled swim in the Selway—it was irrelevant—but I have thought about it from time to time over the years. I have heard and read in magazines of several fly fishermen who have drowned. Not just in the West, either. Last year a man, a canoeist, drowned in the Kennebago, a smallish, friendly (I thought) stream I fish frequently. I know the stretch where he drowned. "How could anyone drown there?" I thought when I read it. I still don't know, but I have come to believe that it may not be as hard to drown as I once imagined, and that it might not have been as easy as I once thought to extricate myself from a particular pool on the Selway without the assistance of that tree, either. The fact was, I was lucky. I still don't know how lucky, but lucky.

In 1989, I took my older boy, Preston, who was then thirteen, out west. It was the first time for him and the first for me since '82, though I had promised myself I wouldn't let that much time pass. Whether he fished or not, I wanted him to see the country.

He loved it all: the way the land opened like the palm of a hand and let you see as far as you could see; a hawk perched on a fence post beside a county road, and the hawk not moving as we drove past; the mountains close and still carrying snow in July; cattle ranging freely across the road; a ghost town, with gas still selling for thirty cents a gallon. These things excited him, and his excitement carried over into the fishing. It was the most enthusiasm he had ever shown for fishing.

It was left for me to remind him not to get *too* excited, not to forget where he was going, and when wading, to watch where he placed each foot, and to remember: the clearest water was the most deceptive. At least with murky water, you knew you didn't know where you were going. Let him draw his own conclusions.

Uncle Harry's Funeral

WHEN STEVE AND I FIRST SAW THE FISH, WE WERE STANDING IN Hal's yard reminiscing about Harry Hall, my great-uncle, Steve's grandfather, whose funeral would be in a few short hours.

It was spring, and the birdsongs, warm air, the scent of fresh grass, jonquils, and forsythia cast a sort of spell on us. The herring had already run; the first peeler crabs had moved inshore, attracting striped bass to the shallows in search of succulent soft crabs—which probably accounted for the flash of silver. A school of stripers—"rock"—had evidently moved into the grassy cove in back of Hal's house, which until two days earlier had been Harry's house. Now it was all Hal's, the farm, the fishing boats, the crab floats, wharf, and oyster shore inside the sand point, where now, it appeared, fish were feeding.

We meandered over toward the shoreline for a better look. A gull dove. We shielded our eyes and studied the situation and came to the same conclusion: Yep, it was a school of rock all right. Wasn't that something? Fresh from the city, with a funeral to attend, we weren't in a "fishing mode." We were still in our city clothes—slacks, sport shirts, and street shoes. Sometimes, as young adults, you just had to accept the fact that there would be times when it wasn't appropriate to go fishing, even when, as it now appeared, fish were practically feeding at your doorstep. So we stood at the edge of the yard, the late-morning sunshine warming our shoulders, and we reminisced about Harry Hall. Wasn't it ironic, we agreed, that all three Hall brothers died in the same year, 1960, and that Harry, the frailest, outlived both his brothers, Eugie and Snowden, Jr.

There were several surviving sisters, but those were the only sons of the original Snowden Hall, who had inherited that farm from a Colonel Dulaney, whose life Hall had saved in the Civil War. He had dragged Dulaney, wounded, from the battlefield, and for his heroism Private Hall was given first a job on that farm and later, for a few hundred dollars, the farm itself: six hundred or so acres of fields, beach, woods, inlets, points, creeks, and two brackish water ponds. This was the place that, no matter how much it eroded (and the acreage had been considerably reduced since Civil War days) or how far we wandered from it, we, like most Halls, considered home.

My favorite recollections of Harry were the times he, Eugie, and Hal would come and visit at my grandfather's house just down the road after a meal, usually at Thanksgiving or Christmas, sometimes just a Sunday dinner. Those three would sit on the sofa in the crowded little dining room, while the rest of us finished eating. Talk would always turn to hunting, fishing, oystering, or crabbing, and usually they'd end up arguing about some seemingly minor detail, such as which way the wind had been blowing that morning on the Great Wicomico River when they caught five thousand dollars worth of croaker in a single fishing; or how many bushels of oysters Hal had nippered up six winters ago; or how many ducks they might have killed, or what kind. But these were not minor details to them, and weather was never small talk to a waterman.

As I recall, Harry never lost an argument. Hal's memory even then wasn't the best, and though Eugie was the best educated, almost a Ph.D., he wasn't the contentious type. But Harry was cantankerous, and his jimmy-jaw gave him a feisty, defiant look. He had a thick shock of black hair that didn't turn gray until his last years. Hal, Harry's son, had the same hair, but his turned gray much sooner, possibly as the result of *being* Harry's son.

Harry was a tough taskmaster, a hard man to please. Even when he was too weak to help Hal fish, Harry kept going out on the *Mary Virginia* to supervise almost until the day he died. Rain or shine, rough or calm, in sickness and in health, come sunup, sometimes before, Harry Hall was onboard the *Mary Virginia*. And he was still in charge, still captain of that boat, and even when he was too short of breath to walk from the house to the dock without stopping to rest, he could still give orders: tighten up that line; tow that skiff closer astern; get that fish slime off that gunwale before somebody slips and falls overboard. What's the matter with you, boy! Hal was in his thirties then, had been fishing all his life and needed no supervision, but I never heard him talk back or lose his temper.

While Steve and I were reminiscing, a few more gulls had moved onto the flats. It wasn't a feeding frenzy by any means, but it was enough to make us nervous. The tide was so high the cove seemed about to overflow its banks and spill onto the lawn. The evidence of subsurface feeding activity was overwhelming: small fish flitting over the surface; gulls hovering nervously; a subtle flash of silver just beneath the surface; the occasional intriguing, deeper swirl, unmistakably a large fish—the flat was like a porridge of fish life, about to come to a boil. It was enough to make any fisherman's mouth water.

"Too bad we've got to go to that funeral," I said.

"Yeah, it is," Steve said.

"Of course, it's only eleven o'clock," I said looking at my watch. The funeral was at two.

Steve scraped at dirt with the toe of his shoe. It had to be his decision. Harry was only my great-uncle; he was Steve's grandfather. Closest of kin had to make the call.

"I doubt that Granddad would be offended if we went fishing before his funeral," he said.

"I wouldn't think so either," I said.

Steve was and is a nice man. Later he became a lawyer, but even in those days he could marshal his arguments well. He certainly convinced me in a very few minutes that we didn't just have the right to go after those fish; we had an obligation. Otherwise, we'd be letting Harry Hall down, maybe the whole family. A few minutes listening to Steve, and we were both a little ashamed it had taken us so long to discern Harry's wishes. He wanted us to get after those fish. In fact, he was probably a little put out with us for standing around, wasting so much time. Soon the tide would change, we'd have missed our chance. "Call yourselves fishermen?" we could hear him say. "Call yourself Halls? What a trifling lot!"

It didn't take long to assemble our gear. There was one spinning rod in Steve's car, another in the dock shed. We didn't bother changing clothes; so what if we got a few fish scales on our good shoes? And who cared if we came to Harry's funeral smelling like fish? What could be more appropriate? Harry probably smelled like fish himself. It would take more than a little formaldehyde to flush the fish out of Harry's system. As long as any portion of Harry Hall existed, on earth or in heaven, whatever form he took, whether flesh and blood or spirit, fish would be a part of him.

Later at his funeral, as if to prove that we had read the signs correctly, not one person suggested we had done anything wrong or disrespectful by fishing right up until a few minutes before the actual services. (And the relatives all knew we'd gone without having to be told. The creek was like an arena, surrounded by houses; each house had a phone; each phone had a party line.)

Most people just wanted to know how many fish we'd caught. (Over a dozen.) What kind? (Rock.) What size? (One to two pounds.) What had we used for bait? (Spoons.) What was the tide? (Flood.) And, of course, the direction of the wind.

Catch-and-Release
Gill Netting

WHEN I WAS GROWING UP, THERE DID NOT SEEM TO BE A CLEAR distinction in our family between commercial fishing and sport-fishing. There was much pleasure to be had in commercial fishing, and hook-and-line-caught fish could also be sold. In the early days on the Chesapeake, there was a commercial hook-and-line fishery for bluefish; members of my own family did it. So it saddens me to see how commercial fishermen have taken such a verbal beating in recent years—from sportfishermen.

Of all forms of commercial fishing, gill netting gets the worst abuse. Meanwhile, the sporting aspects of gill netting, the skill involved, and the esthetics have been badly neglected.

First of all, where to set the net takes the same sort of knowl-edge of seabottom, tides, currents, feeding habits of fish, as is required by flats fishing or, for that matter, fishing rivers and ponds. Furthermore, running a hundred fathoms of monofilament net over the transom of a splintery, wooden skiff takes at least as much skill as a roll cast or double haul. The best system I found was to run the net over the ankle of a rubber boot, but one wrong move and you could snag your toe and go overboard and drown. Fishing the net, whether just overhauling it or pulling it into the boat, takes strength particularly in a breeze, because you're basically dragging the skiff upwind. (Big rigs use motorized winders and reels, which come with their own problems.)

Removing the fish can be easy or hard, depending on what you've caught. Soft fish, spot and menhaden, can be shaken out, but croaker and rock take patience (or you'll slice your fingers and the net) and two hands, which means the net has to be cinched against the gunwale with a knee, while the waves are tossing the boat around and your feet are sliding about on wooden floorboards slick with a slurry of fish slime and sea nettle juice. When fish start flopping about in that mess, your eyes are in real danger.

Then there're the crabs. Hard crabs feed on gilled fish, dead or alive, doesn't seem to matter to a crab. They start with the tail and eat toward the head. A net untended long enough can yield a catch of fish heads attached to skeletons—like fish in Halloween costumes strung together like cutout paper dolls.

Eventually the greedy crabs get tangled in the net. Strands of monofilament catch on the spines of crab shell and in the joints of their many legs. Crabs are irascible by nature—hence the term "crabby"—and a tangled crab is furious and foaming at the mouth like a rabid dog, ready to snap at anything, even a helping hand. It's said that the pincer of a large Jimmy crab can break a finger. I can't say I've ever seen it happen, but I've suffered enough nips, dents, cuts, and bruises from smaller crabs to believe it could. The worst leader knot pales in comparison to a tangle of net around an enraged crab. The only safe solution is to crush the crab with the heel of your boot and shake the remains overboard. I hate doing it—it's cruel and crabs are worth money—but I value my fingers and always suspected I'd have to put them to some use other than gill netting, such as typing or tying flies.

On the other hand, the pleasures of gill netting are considerable. The throb of line, the suspense, the first glimpse of fish are similar to the thrills of hook-and-line fishing. The prettiest gill netting comes in the fall. A net full of fat spot on a sunny day glows in the water like a gold necklace. The absence of sea nettles from the Chesapeake is as much a blessing as the end of black fly season in Maine. And fish don't soften and spoil so fast in the cool fall water, so you don't have to overhaul your net in the middle of the night.

By far the most sporting form of gill netting is "thrash netting," in which an entire cove is cordoned off with net. Ideally, each end of the net is so close to shore that the fish can't swim around it. Usually the top-line corks are exposed like a long, curved row of bobbers or strike indicators. Once the set is made, the enclosed area is thrashed, traditionally with a long, flexible branch, a "thrash pole," but any form of ruckus will do—propwash, an oar banged against the bottom of the boat, anything to drive the fish toward deep water. When the panicky fish hit the net, the corks dance, sink, and resurface. It is quite exciting. You can even release your catch alive and unharmed. Granted, it isn't common practice, but it can be done. I've done it.

One hot August afternoon in the late sixties, when striped bass were still plentiful, I decided to take advantage of an extremely high tide and cast a few soft crabs on the grassy flats back of Hal's house. My skiff stayed at my uncle's dock because, well, it was his skiff, but I had claimed it for the summer. I had removed the middle seat and all else except a single oar, dip net, gas tank, one life jacket, and a rusted knife stuck into the stern seat. Except for my spinning rod, it looked like a small but serious workboat, which it was. It smelled like one, too. In the bow, a mound of gill net covered by a canvas tarpaulin emitted a perfume of fish, crab, and seaweed—the Essence of the Chesapeake.

I cranked the Evinrude and eased the skiff into the creek toward Hal's crab floats. In those days Hal was still fishing traps. The fish and hard crabs he sold immediately, but the peeler crabs—those about to shed into more valuable soft crabs—he kept in a string of floats between his house and my uncle's. Hal and I had an agreement whereby I was entitled to the dead soft crabs. The trouble was, death of a soft crab can be very difficult to determine. Soft crabs don't move much. They *can't*—they've got no skeleton. They just lie around waiting for their shell to harden. It's hard to tell if they're dead or alive. And it's impossible with bursters, which are crabs in the act of shedding, a painfully slow process to begin with, like removing a cold, wet foot from a boot several sizes too small. I suppose if I'd had all day, I could have made a more careful assessment of the situation, but I didn't. The tide was falling, so I did the best I could. I scooped up three or four moribund crabs, cranked the engine, and scooted around the point to the shallow cove of eelgrass and oyster shore.

I cut the engine, and the boat drifted in a light breeze. The cove heaved and sighed from a slight ground swell. I baited a single unweighted hook with a hunk of crab and slung it toward shore, where it slowly sank. Before it hit bottom, the bait and my line began moving diagonally away. I tried to set the hook, felt a brief resistance, then nothing. I reeled in; no bait. I added a smaller piece of crab, slightly exposed the point of the hook, and slung it once again, and once again something moved the line through the water, quickly this time, but again when I tried to set the hook, there was no fish. It happened time and again: The fish would pick up the bait, swim with it, but wouldn't solidly take it. It was very frustrating.

I sat on the gunwale in the hot sun trying to decide what to do. I wanted to see a fish. I don't mind losing a fish once I've gotten a good look, although sometimes a good look only makes it worse. Still, all in all, I'd rather know the truth. Half the thrill of fishing is the mystery: strange unseen creatures coming from the deep. This cove connected to the Bay, which connected to open ocean linking all continents—theoretically it could have been *anything* taking my bait. But once I finished pondering the wonder of it all, the many possibilities, I wanted to solve the mystery. I wanted a damn answer! At times like these, it's handy to have a gill net around. Ninety-nine times out of a hundred I don't have one. That day I did.

I checked out the dimensions of the cove; I couldn't quite enclose it entirely, but I could come very close. And in no time at all, I had that net running out over the stern, the sinkers making that lovely hollow, rattling sound of lead on wood that they make when there's no rubber boot to run them over. (Which made me wonder, why didn't I just tack a piece of rubber over the transom and forget the boot? Probably because Hal didn't; if he didn't do it, there had to be a reason.)

It was a good set: Both anchors were practically onshore, connected by a smooth curve of corks that to my eyes was every bit as lovely as the tight loop of a well-cast fly line. It's all a matter of perspective, point of view. (My sister's friend, Collin, a fish spotter for the menhaden fleet, once showed me aerial photos he'd made of striker boats surrounding a huge school of fish. It was beautiful—the dark mass of menhaden, a delicate arc of net, the bay as luminous and green as a bonefish flat.)

The skiff was inside the enclosure when I cranked the engine. As I spun tight circles, I pounded the boat bottom with an oar, making a considerable racket. I kept my eyes on the corks, which rose and fell from the boat wake, but those nearest the channel darted and dipped when the fish hit at full speed. Then the corks quivered as the gilled fish shimmied and wriggled. I motored to one end of the net, cut the engine, and began fishing the net as quickly as possible, before the fish suffocated. It was a while before I came to the first fish, a rock about eighteen inches long, still frisky and alive. Quickly I plied the monofilament from his gill plates and released the fish on the bay side of the net. I didn't want to catch him twice.

I caught about two dozen rock, all identical in size and none seriously injured. I let them go. I had solved the mystery, and yet I hadn't hurt the fish. All in all it was a very satisfying experience. I sat back on the gunwale to enjoy the moment. I had fooled the fish, and as far as I was concerned, it didn't matter how I'd done it. Fishing was fishing. I had simply used the tools at my disposal—another triumph of human resourcefulness. Three cheers for man's ingenuity!

The trouble was, Hal had witnessed the whole scene from his bedroom window. My commotion had awakened him from his afternoon nap. Groggy with sleep and the heavy, wet summer heat, he wasn't sure what he had seen. He saw me make the set; he saw me picking fish; but when he walked down to the end of his dock and beckoned me over to see what I'd caught, there weren't any fish in sight, just a lone limp crab crawling feebly toward shade. Hal craned his neck, searching the nooks and crannies for fish, his leathery, lined face a portrait of confusion and fatigue.

Like a fool, I was still feeling proud of my "accomplishment" and was almost boastful when I told him what I'd done: "I caught about two dozen rock, but I turned 'em all loose."

He looked at me in dismay. "What'd you do that for?"

I shrugged. "I didn't need 'em," I said, no longer boastful. It was slowly sinking in that I wasn't the hero I thought I was, at least not in Hal's eyes, and at the moment his were the only ones that counted.

He shook his head. "Just throwing money overboard," he said, voice trailing off. He simply couldn't believe that anyone, much less a member of his own family, would turn loose fish that sold for forty-five cents a pound. Just before he turned to walk back to the house, he gave me a look that said clearly I did not have, and would not ever have, what it took to be a *real* commercial fisherman.

I cranked the engine and motored slowly across the creek. I stopped at Hal's ripe peeler float, threw the engine out of gear, and gently took the one surviving crab and worked him back and forth in the water, trying to revive him. His back fins flickered weakly. I thought he'd be all right. I headed back toward my uncle's dock.

So I guess there was a distinction, after all, between commercial fishing and sportfishing. I just hadn't seen it clearly until that day, when I saw it in Hal's eyes and heard it in his voice. Commercial fishing could be fun, but it wasn't meant to be a game. It was serious business, life or death for the fish and the fishermen. And people, least of all city people, ought not to forget it. Hal was right about me, of course. I didn't have what it took to be a real commercial fisherman, and I never would have it. After a while I stopped wanting it, but that was years later.

Conflict at Cayman Brac

THE FOUR FISH WEREN'T LARGE BY TARPON STANDARDS, ABOUT fifty pounds, but they were tantalizingly close, no more than twenty feet from the end of the dock. No stalking would be required, no stealth, just a flip cast upcurrent, let the fly drift down, and boom, simple as that. Unfortunately, it wasn't to be. A fresh sign stated in no uncertain terms, "Fishing from the Pier Is Strictly Prohibited." Cayman Brac is a dive site. Divers and snorkelers from all over the world come to experience the gorgeous coral and exotic tropical species, but only a few misguided souls come to fish.

To an outsider it might seem that divers and fishermen have much in common, namely, fish, but such is not the case. Divers and fishermen see marine life in radically different ways. As best I can tell, divers view the underwater world as a museum cum petting zoo. Fish are to be admired and occasionally touched or fed. This bridging of the gap between species appears to be a very emotional experience for divers, but if a fisherman closes the same gap with a fly connected to a piece of line, it is a sinister act demonstrating man's cruelty, even if he releases his catch. Of course, if a fish kills another fish, that's OK; that's just nature at work, man evidently no longer being part of nature.

During the daylight hours, the divers and I would go our separate ways; I would stalk the shallows for bonefish, and the divers would head to deeper water. But come evening, we'd all congregate on the long pier that extended far into the lagoon. Small fish would be drawn by spotlights that shone into the water, and they in turn would attract tarpon, which held in tidal current like trout in a stream.

Often a few divers would enter the water to observe the action; other divers would stand, observe, and offer commentary. I couldn't help but overhear their conversations, and their attitude toward the fish struck me as condescending. They spoke of tarpon as if they were manatees—docile, innocuous creatures. They seemed to have no idea of the tarpon's latent power or of its diabolical ability to tease and torment fishermen, to destroy tackle. I got the distinct feeling that divers wouldn't truly appreciate a tarpon until they saw one hooked.

I'd never hooked one myself, but I'd seen the videos and fishing shows, and once, riding through the Florida Keys on Route 1, crossing a channel, I saw a huge tarpon leap out of the water for no obvious reason, glimmer in the sunlight, then fall back with a huge splash. It looked like a chamber of commerce ad for the species and the Keys. But I'd never really had a chance to fish for them, and I still didn't.

Cayman Brac was doubly frustrating: I couldn't fish, and I had to listen to patronizing comments about tarpon. There was no rule against wade fishing in the lagoon, but the water was so deep that even if I'd waded up to my chest, the fish would've still been out of range. The fly fisherman's paradox: The deeper you wade, the less line you can handle, because your backcast will hit the water. There's a point at which it's not worth wading farther. Probably this point could be calculated for each person—as a function of water depth, height of fisherman, upper-body strength, and so on—and taught in fly-fishing schools. Once you've reached a certain depth, there's no point wading deeper, and it's dangerous. You lose your footing. So don't do it!

After three nights of tarpon watching, my frustration was reaching the breaking point. On the fourth night a stranger sauntered out onto the dock. It was obvious at first glance that he wasn't a diver. I recognized the flinty, gunslinger glint in his eye when he spotted the large fish, the fidgety, nervous movements of his hand. He was a fellow predator, a fisherman. He looked at the spectators in disbelief, extended his hands as if to say, "Why isn't somebody doing something about those fish?"

I couldn't help but smile. He noticed, and I nodded toward the sign.

"What about wading out?" he asked. "Is there a rule against that?"

"Not that I know of, but it's too deep for me to get in range with a fly rod."

But this fellow—his name was Warren—was a spin fisherman. He walked back down the dock, studied the depth of water and slope of the bottom. "I can get a large Rapala out there without any trouble," he said matter-of-factly. "The only problem is, once I'm in the water, I won't be able to see the fish."

"Well," I said, "I believe I could help with that." I already liked Warren. I liked how he approached fish as a problem to be solved. I liked his confidence, and what I knew he must have overcome, because he had a slightly withered left arm, a congenital injury, his wife, Helen, later explained. His right arm, however, looked very strong, not Popeyesque, but definitely hypertrophied and capable, I imagined, of long, powerful casts.

So the next evening, while the divers were still digesting their food and before it was fully dark, we took our positions. I stood at the end of the pier, acting as forward observer. Helen stood with me to watch and offer moral support. Warren waited in the shallows for the lights that would bring the fish.

Soon a few divers straggled from the dining room, rubbing their stomachs, lugging their gear. Finally the sun set, the lights came on, and out of nowhere four tarpon materialized in the feeding lanes. The divers began suiting up, donning wet suits, checking their regulators and air tanks.

"If I were you, I wouldn't go in just yet," I said. I pointed in the direction of Warren, now wading into the deeper water, arms held high, the heavy Rapala dangling from the end of his spinning rod like a ripe fruit bending a branch.

"What's he doing?" a diver asked.

"Looks to me like he's going fishing," I said.

"Here?"

"So it would appear."

There was desultory grumbling among the divers.

Meanwhile Warren had waded as far as he could and was awaiting instructions. "Four fish," I shouted. "About twenty feet out, thirty feet to the right of this corner."

He reached back; his rod bent sharply, then whipped forward and launched the Rapala like a rocket. It appeared to be on line; then the breeze lifted the lure like a nine-iron shot that ballooned, hovered, and fell softly, short and behind the fish.

"Fifteen feet short, fifteen left," I shouted. "There's more wind up there than I realized."

Warren slowly reeled in the lure. It took a long time. More divers arrived; they grew restive and surly.

"Try the other side," I said, motioning to the dark side of the dock.

A male diver glared. "We need the light," he said.

"So do we," I said. These people had had the run of this place long enough, I reasoned. They'd grown smug and complacent, and in all likelihood that complacency had been transmitted like an infection to the fish. The way I saw it, Warren and I were a tonic for those fish, an antidote to the divers. We celebrated the very wildness the divers would domesticate. Tarpon are simply not meant to be pets.

Meanwhile, the fish had drifted back slightly. I relayed the new coordinates, and Warren launched another cast. Once again the lure fell short and to the left. "I pulled it," he said.

"No problem," said I. "We've got all night." There was a groan from the divers.

"The fish have drifted back," I yelled to Warren. "They're right off the end of the dock. Make the same cast, but twenty feet farther. The current will do the rest."

He did. The beauty of fly casting is a matter of public record, widely celebrated in magazines, books, videos, and even a major motion picture. But whoever thought of spin casting as beautiful? How many great spin-fishing movies have been made? Well, Warren's Rapala sailing like a cruise missile through the soft night air, trailing a graceful arc of monofilament, illuminated by the orange light of the setting sun, was every bit as beautiful to my eyes as any cast Brad Pitt ever made. Warren's Rapala settled softly as a seagull onto the water, its quiet plop undetected by the feeding tarpon fifteen feet downcurrent.

Without turning around or taking my eyes off the lure, I gave Warren the OK sign. As the Rapala drifted toward the waiting tarpon, even the divers were silent and attentive.

The take, though no surprise, was so violent that we all jumped back from the rail. The lead fish took the Rapala and erupted from the water, rose several feet into the air, then wrenched his head one way, then the other, his scales rippling like roof shingles in a strong wind. The twenty-pound-test line popped like a rifle shot, and the expensive lure sailed far out into the lagoon. The fish collapsed back into the water with all the grace of an outhouse toppled by a tornado.

"Son of bitch!" a diver said. It sounded like a compliment. It certainly should've been. A compliment to the fish. I was proud of that fish, and proud of Warren and even a little proud of myself. Warren and I had given that fish a chance to express itself, and illogical as it may have been, I could imagine the fish was grateful for the opportunity to kick up its heels in public. One thing I was sure of, those divers would never see tarpon in quite the same benign light again. How could they look at a tarpon without remembering the night one exploded under their noses? From now on, I hoped, they would handle tarpon with more respect and maybe, just maybe, with even a little concern for their own safety. Well, we can all dream, and win or lose, we can always declare victory and go home. Which was exactly what I did.

I called it a win, and without saying another word—the tarpon did my talking for me—I took Helen's arm and escorted her back down the pier toward her waiting husband, who stood silhouetted against the evening sky, his spinning rod cradled like a carbine in his arms.

Fishing Partners

SELECTING A FISHING PARTNER IS TRICKY BUSINESS. SO MANY forces have to align themselves for the process to work. Ultimately it comes down to chemistry, timing, and luck.

My first freshwater fishing partner was a wiry Mainer by the name of Mahlon, a hunter and a woodsman. He even fished a little, but once on Spencer Stream in the middle of a caddis hatch, he found a logging chain and became so excited he quit fishing and started lugging the chain back to the truck. The chain was enormous, each link about the size of a man's fist. He had trouble dragging the heavy chain and carrying his fly rod at the same time. Would I be so kind, he wondered, as to carry his rod for him? No, as a matter of fact, I wouldn't, but I did suggest where he might carry it. "I came to fish," I said, "not to collect junk." I could see that hurt; it was meant to, but he had struck the first blow by insulting the stream, the trout, and therefore, me.

Another time on Parker Pond he jumped ship to investigate a loon's nest. Normally, I'm tolerant of that sort of thing. I realize, fish do not exist in a vacuum, but in a great natural arena of birds, flowers, deer, and so on, and that when the fishing is slow, we admire these lovely creations and say things such as, "Well, it's just nice to be out on a day like this." But that day the fishing wasn't slow; it was excellent, and you simply don't neglect good fishing for loons.

Later that day Mahlon and I switched positions; I was in the stern, paddling, while he sat in the bow supposedly fishing but, in fact, still admiring wildlife. Three times a sizable smallmouth rose to Mahlon's popper, and three times Mahlon missed the strike because he wasn't watching the popper. "Will you please pay attention!" I said after the third miss.

Whereupon he turned and smiled—he's a nice fellow—and said, "Don't get so excited. It don't make that much difference to me."

"In that case, you sit back here," I said.

And he did. I paddled ashore, we switched positions, and he never sat in the bow again. In fact, even though we remained friends until he moved upcountry, we didn't fish much together after that.

Mike was not a friend. He was the husband of my wife's friend. I took him fishing as a favor to them. Mike was a chef, and even in his fishing gear he resembled one. When he plopped his portly frame into the bow of my canoe, we bulldozed through the water like a barge. He was a bait fisherman but was glad to try fly fishing, so I took him to a favorite pond, one I fished often and felt protective about. Usually I wouldn't keep a fish unless it was injured already, but—and this is where I went wrong—I hadn't told Mike that.

Often these inaugural outings aren't successful, but this one was, and soon Mike hooked a nice two-pound smallmouth. It ran and jumped, did everything a good fish was supposed to do, but was well hooked and was soon in hand. Mike wanted to keep the fish. I said fine and strung it up. It was a good fish, his first on a fly rod; he had a right to feel proud, and I was a little proud myself that I could put a fly rod in his hand and show him fish. Also, I hate to be too rigid about catch and release; they're just fish, and human relationships come first. Up to a point. Then he caught another, smaller, fish and kept that too. Fine, that pond could handle the loss of two fish. Mike was excited; I was pleased.

Afterward I took him home. He ran into his house with the fish, as excited as a kid. A few moments later he ran back out, still carrying the fish, which he handed to me. "I just wanted to show her the larger one," he said. "I kept them for you."

I could see he meant well; he meant them as a gift, to thank me for taking him, and if I were a nicer person, I would've said, "You're welcome," but I couldn't and didn't. "I wish you'd told me you didn't want the fish," I said, eyeing the two carcasses.

"I wanted them for you."

"Next time let me know, OK?"

But of course, there wasn't any next time. Something always seemed to come up, and then he moved back to North Carolina.

Then came Phil, who didn't kill fish—too messy to clean— but he loved to go, and we caught many fish together. The next year he bought an Orvis rod, and I thought, "Well, now, this is getting serious." Then I found out he had four deer rifles, even though he'd never killed a deer; a Troy-Bilt tiller for a tiny garden; three bicycles, but only a single car for him and his wife. Soon transportation became a problem; he needed rides back and forth. Then he began having trouble deciding how best to spend his time, whether to ride his bike, plant flowers, or fish, as if these activities were of equal importance. The second year, we fished only a few times together, and last year only once, just enough to justify the rod, new canoe, and outboard. The last I knew, he was pricing waders.

Cherie was the least likely prospect for a fishing partner. Gender wasn't the issue. One of my favorite fishing companions is my sister Ida, who at the age of fourteen was independent on the water and now fishes commercially.

The problem with Cherie was age and inexperience. She was thirty and had never fished. Her husband didn't fish. Her father didn't fish; he sailed. Her brother sailed. She sailed, my brother sails, and sailors don't make good fishermen. As a rule, sailors take up fishing as an excuse to buy another boat. So one winter evening, when Cherie asked when I was going to take her fishing, I said, "Preferably after the snow melts." Spring seemed infinitely far away. If she was still interested then, we'd see.

By spring she'd read two fly-fishing books, fitted herself with boots, had practiced casting with a borrowed rod, and had even taught herself a few knots. She was raring to go. We started with smallmouth bass. If smallmouth didn't excite her, I wanted to know, and I wanted to know soon.

Our first trip was a week too early on a cold, windy day, and the one fish I caught was so lethargic he fought like an ice cube, then died before I could even release him. Cherie caught nothing, but she didn't complain about the cold or the poor fishing. "It was still fun," she said, as she helped lug the canoe to the truck. She's tall and athletic, also blonde, blue-eyed, and attractive, which in fishing can be counterproductive, leading to too much concern about appearance, hair, and apparel, how waders fit or which hat to wear. With Cherie this was not a problem. Her waders fit fine; ridiculous hats agreed with her; she still managed to look good; but more importantly, she was a trouper.

Finally real spring arrived, in Maine a thin sliver of time sandwiched between mud season and summer. One warm, calm evening we fished the rocky, empty islands of Parker Pond. In the sunlight, there's a Caribbean clarity to Parker Pond, whereby the mossy, submerged boulders resemble emerald-colored coral heads. Tall pines usually hold at least one pair of nesting ospreys. And the island's shorelines always hold fish. We caught plenty, but the last one was after dark, by the light of a full moon. The fish took Cherie's popper, jumped, shook, and the spray sparkled in the moonlight like diamonds.

Next it was summer, and time for Morse Pond and largemouth bass. Morse Pond is a quiet, carry-in place with no boat launch and not one camp on its entire circumference. The shoreline is wooded, except for a meadow of a dairy farm. The farmhouse sits far up on a hill; there're no people noises, and the lowing cattle just add to the tranquility. The pond itself is L-shaped, shallow, fertile with lily pads, cattails, reeds, and an extraordinary abundance of insects. Feeding bass often leap out of the water for damselflies, dragonflies, and the caddisflies that hatch in huge numbers at dark. Many of my fish are taken covering rises, which are more like a hand grenade going off in the water than like a typical trout rise. The bass are not subtle and usually aren't fussy. Even if they're feeding on damselflies or caddisflies, they'll take a popping bug.

Cherie loved the fishing, and she appreciated the solitude, the silence, the wildlife, the lily pads, loons, turtles that lined up on fallen logs, and startled black ducks that leapt from the cattails like jack-in-the-boxes. She loved it all, and she caught a lot of fish. Because Morse Pond is close, we fished it frequently. We could sneak out after work, fish the long summer twilights until the edge of dark, when Morse Pond truly came alive with leaping bass, caddisflies, mayflies, and mosquitoes—a rich biological brew. The last fish would usually come after dark, as I slowly paddled back along the shoreline and Cherie fished by sound and feel.

But soon, too soon, it was fall, and time to move on to the Kennebago for landlocked salmon. It's a ninety-minute drive to the Kennebago, then a two-mile bike ride, then a hike over a trail littered with fallen timber—dry kill—that forces you off the trail into fields of boulders, alders, prickly spruce, and fir. The footing is unreliable, and the fishing is hit or miss. The day our first time out was bright and sunny, the worst possible conditions for salmon. The radiant foliage did not console me. Cherie never once complained about the walking, the fishing, or me, a veritable Job.

And then, near midday, at a rather unspectacular, shallow pool, in bright sunlight, a salmon materialized out of ledge and shadow, took my fly, and streaked toward the tail of the pool. If he'd continued into the heavy water, he would've easily gotten loose, but it goes against a salmon's nature to swim downstream in fall. He raced back to the head of the pool and leaped high into the air, shiny and silver, right in front of our eyes. "He's beautiful," Cherie yelled, as excitedly as if the fish had been on her line instead of mine.

I lost track of how often the fish jumped, but he soon wore himself out, and I slid him into the shallows and netted him.

Legally, you could keep one fish. "Do you want to keep him?" I asked, as I measured him at eighteen inches.

"Not if it's a female."

"It's a male." I knew she wanted to take a fish back to her husband. Who wouldn't? It's part of how we justify our time away from home.

Cherie was quiet for a moment, then said, "Oh, let him go. He's too pretty to kill."

"Thank Cherie for your life," I said, as I revived and then released the fish. He shot away and disappeared in water so shallow it hardly seemed adequate to conceal such a bright, shining fish, but such are the mysteries of fish and rivers.

Cherie and I sat in the warm sun, feeling pleased with ourselves. A single fish can do that. If it's the right fish, it can change

a day from miserable to memorable. A relationship can be transformed too—from acquaintance or casual friendship to something
more, a partnership. I was sure at that moment, that morning, that
I had found a fishing partner for a lifetime. I couldn't have been
more wrong.

We fished together a few more years, and then Cherie
betrayed me: She went and hatched her own little fishing partner,
Luke. He's almost six now, elfin, adorable, and I had the privilege
of participating in his very first fishing trip, on Morse Pond, but it
was a bittersweet experience, because I knew for me it was the
beginning of the end. My days as Cherie's fishing partner were
numbered, and Luke numbered them. So I hope you appreciate
what you've got, Luke. I don't know what she's like as a mother,
but take it from me, you'll be hard-pressed to find a better fishing
partner.

Golf Versus Fishing

IN THE SUMMER OF 1996 MY FOURTEEN-YEAR-OLD SON, EVAN, discovered golf. By the next summer he was addicted to the game, and I felt like a failure as a father. As a reformed golfer, I was well aware of the sport's sordid allure and felt I should have warned him.

As an innocent ten-year-old I was introduced to golf by an older boy, Jimmy Flippen, who lived across the street and was already so enamored of the sport that he had turned his own backyard into a miniature golf course. Later he won a number of amateur championships and sired a son who turned professional, but before the son, before the titles, there was me.

In those days, I did enjoy the game, but even more I enjoyed the camaraderie, loitering around the local pro shop, swapping lies with my friends, soaking up golf lore from the local pros, a couple of whom had actually played the PGA Tour. There we sat, day after sweltering summer day, sipping our R.C. Colas, lunching on Moon Pies and peanuts, listening to tales of Hogan, Snead, Demaret, Mike Souchak, and later, Arnold Palmer, who'd played on the same Wake Forest team as Frankie Jones, a local boy, and where Frank Merchant, one of our gang, would later go on scholarship. In fact, our group eventually produced half a dozen college golfers, three professionals, two Virginia State Amateur Champions, and one fly fisherman.

I had lost interest in golf long before I discovered fly fishing, hadn't played for years, and didn't even like my fishing colleagues to know I was a former golfer. Even though no less a person than Lefty Kreh has likened fly fishing to golf (I wish he hadn't), fishing is far more serious than golf. Fishing is more than a game or sport. Fishing is about life and death. It cuts to the mysterious core of life and connects us to our primitive hunter-gatherer heritage, and yet invites us to transcend our primitive selves and, of all things, release our catch. Golf invites us to drink and gamble.

Except that Evan didn't see it that way. He saw golf as pure, unadulterated fun. Not only that, "but golf is something we could do together," he said, batting his cute blue eyes.

"We can fish together too," said I.

His eyes turned cold as ice cubes. "Fishing is boring," he said.

I learned from my first nonfishing son that the worst mistake a father can make is to coerce a son into fishing. It ruins the fishing and doesn't help the father–son relationship.

So in the summer of '96 I dusted off my '54 Spaulding irons and my '72 MacGregor woods, built when woods were actually made of wood, before graphite, titanium, and all the other hi-tech gimmickry I found so offensive (in golf but, paradoxically, in fishing I have lovingly embraced each technological advance, from graphite—so easy to cast, it cured my bursitis—to braided butt leaders, to bead heads, epoxy bodies, sparkle hair, mylar, and fluorocarbon).

Evan is left-handed, with a long, fluid golf swing, lovely to look at even before it was polished and finished, but difficult to control. Still, the potential was obvious, and on those occasional shots when the potential became reality, Evan's face glowed with the pleasure of a perfectly struck shot. Sadly, in golf perfectly struck shots don't count for much; it's putting and chipping that lead to scoring. I knew in time he would learn, and once he appreciated the fundamental unfairness of the game—a two-foot putt could undo four hundred yards of superb play—maybe he would look elsewhere for outdoor fun. He might even come to realize that even a fishless day astream offers any number of deep, abiding pleasures unrelated to number and size of fish caught. In fishing, you don't have to keep score. In fact, you shouldn't. Scoring obscures the true joys of fishing. Of course, it wasn't to be.

I am by training an M.D., and it is my medical opinion that there is a fishing gene. It not only makes sense; I've seen it in action. How else to explain the simple biological fact that in some people the mere sight of a fish produces an outpouring of adrenaline and in others there is no reaction? None. My children lack the fishing gene; for that matter, so does my brother, but my sister has it in spades (likewise she and I have the same hair and eye color, dark brown, whereas my brother has the blue eyes and light brown hair of our nonfishing father).

I cannot bring myself to believe there is a golf gene. Biologically it makes no sense. There's no survival advantage, whereby fishing skills were once vital to our species. And yet, there was no denying that a well-struck golf shot lived on in Evan's mind as vividly as a leaping salmon did in mine. Riding down the highway, Evan would pass time by picturing how a three wood shot would have to be shaped to fit the curve of road. To Evan, every meadow was a potential fairway; every stream or pond, rather than a habitat for fish, represented a water hazard. He studied golf catalogs as lovingly as I ogled those from Orvis and L. L. Bean. He even memorized the prices. If only he'd applied the same diligence to his schoolwork! He did apply the obsession: Every

English paper was on golf; for physics he built a Stimp meter, to measure the speed of greens; and on "Job Shadow Day," he visited the local driving range, where later he took his first summer job. In Evan's empire all roads led to golf, and eventually, inevitably, they led to Myrtle Beach.

To Maine golfers, Myrtle Beach is Mecca. It is relatively inexpensive and reachable by car. It offers a hundred courses and innumerable golf packages all neatly presented in a single catalog, which included color photographs of the accommodations and of the golf courses—lovely blue water and pristine white sand traps lining lush green fairways that led to even lusher, beautifully manicured greens. That catalog spent the fall of '96 on our dinner table beside Evan's place. Its pages became worn, tattered, and food-stained, as Evan mentally played each course, planning his strategy—where he'd place his drive, his approach shots—much as I used to lie awake the night before a fishing trip, deciding how to approach a river, which pools to fish, which flies to use.

When February finally arrived, a snowstorm delayed our trip one day. Evan was frantic, but the next day we drove hard and made it to Virginia. Too many memories for me in Virginia, but this trip, I had to shelve my past and see the South anew through Evan's eyes. The first bare ground was exciting—we were tired of Maine's white on white, and water in its liquid state was cause for a minor celebration. Then green grass and trees with leaves; how remarkable! And then, in South Carolina, not far from our destination, we saw an actual living palm tree. I thought Evan would explode. He'd never seen a palm tree except on television.

Soon reality, in the form of golf, set in. Many of Myrtle Beach's golf courses are merely real estate developments with fairways running through them, often rather narrow fairways. Golf is secondary to the real business of selling house lots. On some holes it's as if you're driving down a canyon of houses or condominiums, a claustrophobic situation for the novice or even intermediate golfer. The proximity of those houses did not help our rusty golf swings. In fact, on our first day Evan's drives seemed magnetically attracted to houses, patios, and roofs.

Another factor not widely advertised is the assembly line quality of Myrtle Beach golf: Golfers are dispatched in carts at close and regular intervals. Golf course revenues are a function of number of rounds played, which is determined, in part, by speed of play. Marshals prowl the course in carts hustling people along—cordially, of course, this is the South—but the ubiquitous presence of these marshals contributed to the tension. As did my efforts to help Evan with his push-fade-slice; whatever you called it, my swing tips only made it worse and irritated Evan. His irritation, in turn, irritated me. Why couldn't he correct this problem? Why wouldn't he listen? Never mind he was a teenager and a novice golfer.

Three days of this, and our nerves were frayed and our vacation, our whole relationship, seemed in jeopardy. On day three I saw a sign—not a portent, but an actual sign. We were walking off the eighteenth green at Deer Track Golf Course, sullenly heading to the parking lot, another sullen dinner awaited us, another sullen shopping trip for golf balls—we were going through a dozen a day—when I looked up and saw the sign, "Home of the Perfect Swing Golf School, Ted Frick, Director." We took a sharp left and followed the arrows to the pro shop, where behind the counter stood Mr. Frick himself.

I introduced myself and briefly outlined the problem: Evan's drives were going dead left. We couldn't correct it on our own. "We need help," I said. Evan stood somberly to the side.

Mr. Frick is a medium-sized man, early to midthirties, I would guess, with sandy brown hair, a soft southern accent, and a compassionate manner that every teacher ought to have, every physician too, I suppose, and every father. Mr. Frick looked outside; it was almost dark. "A little late for tonight," he said.

"What about tomorrow morning?" I asked, hopefully.

"We've got golf school at nine."

"He really needs to get a lesson," I said. "We both need for him to get a lesson."

"Can you get here early?"

"You name the time."

"Seven A.M.?"

"We'll be here." Even Evan, who viewed sleeping late on his vacation as an inalienable right, didn't argue. "And thank you very much for fitting us in." I said. "I really do appreciate it." He had no idea how much.

Dinner was better that night. It was the same cafeteria food we'd been eating all week, but now we had hope; help was on the way.

The sun was barely up the next morning when we arrived at the practice range. Dew was on the grass; it was quiet except for a few crows cawing from the nearby pines. It was peaceful, pastoral; crows always evoked Kilmarnock, the Chesapeake.

Ted Frick assembled his video equipment as efficiently as a radiologist. Evan loosened up. Then, as Evan hit balls, Ted filmed him from two angles at high speed. For once, I was hoping Evan would hit his patented push-fade; there's nothing worse than a patient whose signs of illness disappear in the doctor's office. Luckily Evan obliged.

Then Ted called Evan and me over and reviewed the films. It reminded me of viewing a barium swallow or coronary angiogram: The first part was normal—the stance, grip, and take-away were fine—but on the downswing, there, plain as day, was the lesion. "See how your hips slide instead of rotate," Ted said softly. "See how the hands don't turn over?" Evan saw; we both did. "The ball *has* to go left," Ted said. "It's got no choice." He played and replayed that segment. In slow motion it was so obvious. (If only the rest of our lives could be replayed in slow motion, our arguments and love affairs, so we could edit, revise, and repair.)

Ted gave Evan a few simple exercises to do to get his hips and hands working together. He even had a metal frame to help guide his swing, sort of a supportive brace for a sprained golf swing. Then he had Evan hit balls again. This time every shot took a different trajectory. Some went straight; a few lifted and started left—reminiscent of his old shot—then miraculously turned slowly in midflight with a gentle draw. It was all I could do to keep from giving Ted a hug. Put simply, in one hour he saved our week, and even now Evan benefits from that lesson.

That was February of '97. By the end of the summer of '97, his first full season of play, Evan's handicap was 14. The next year at Myrtle Beach, Evan was one of the better golfers we saw. The problem was all the hackers and duffers slowing us down. We tried to be as compassionate with them as Ted Frick had been with us. It was more than golf Frick taught.

At the end of the next summer of '98, Evan's handicap was 9, and soccer, which he'd played since age six, was a thing of the past. Golf is a fall sport in Maine, and Evan is a golfer. It is as much a part of his identity, of who he is, as fishing is of mine.

As usual, his first school assignment was to describe his summer. He wrote, in part, "The best part of my summer was just being at the golf course almost every day, even though I wasn't always playing. The smell, view, and simple golf chat sunk in enough to keep me satisfied throughout the monotonous Maine winter, when all I can do is fantasize about being on the links."

"The smell, view, and simple golf chat . . ." Boy, did that ring a bell. Not of my golfing past, but of my fishing present. If it's possible to enjoy fishing without catching a fish—and we all know it is—why shouldn't it be possible to enjoy golf without striking a ball? Obviously, for some it is. Evan is among them. I don't fully understand it, but neither do I feel like a failure anymore.

Revisiting golf through Evan made me realize it wasn't golf, per se, that I objected to. The game itself is intriguing even now; it is mysterious, and frustrating, and, I still think, in many ways unfair. But it is also, if not taken too seriously, fun, and ultimately it is imperfectible, which keeps it interesting. If it is true that "we never step into the same river twice," it is also true that we never play the same golf course twice. A course is constantly changing. The weather changes it. The seasons, the wind, course conditions, and every minor variation of one shot changes the shot that follows.

My main objection, I finally realized, wasn't to the game itself, but to the setting in which I learned it, the South in the fifties. It was too private, too privileged, too racially and religiously segregated. In Maine golf is more egalitarian. Private courses are the minority. Evan's home course is blue-collar; jeans and T-shirts are just fine. Greens fees are generally affordable. There're no ethnic barriers. It's golf as it should be, the game and nothing but the game. Of course, it's still not fishing.

This spring, my elder nonfishing son, Preston, graduated from college, returned home, and of all things, took up golf. It had nothing to do with his brother. His old high school friends had taken up the game. So he bought a set of used clubs and off he went. Preston, though plenty athletic, lacks the fluid swing of his younger brother. At the moment, at least, he's a hacker, and it was several months before he was even willing to play with us. And then he did.

Maybe you had to have seen the fights those two boys had growing up to appreciate the rapport they had on the golf course: Evan trying to help his older brother; his older brother actually allowing him to help; and then, the two of them actually complimenting each other on good shots, or even shots that weren't so good.

At the end of the fall, when I looked back, I was chagrined at how little fishing I'd done, as opposed to how much golf I'd played. I guess it's a sign of age, but I finally had to admit that—with all due respect to the rivers and ponds and especially to the fish—golfing with my sons was more fun than fishing without them. For that matter, tennis probably would have been, and I really dislike tennis.

Home

HOME IS AN INTERESTING CONCEPT THAT IN MY CASE ALWAYS involves water and usually includes fish.

The first place that ever felt like home to me was our family's farm on the Chesapeake Bay near Kilmarnock, Virginia. The land was sold to my great-grandfather, Snowden C. Hall, by Col. Richard Dulaney, whose life Private Hall saved in the Civil War. My great-grandfather was later shot in the face by Yankees, but he survived and sired three sons and four daughters. The sons inherited the farm.

Even though I wasn't actually raised there and never spent more than one summer on that farm, no place felt as much like home to me as Kilmarnock, and no place matched my concept of paradise as closely: several hundred acres of woods and fields, two large ponds, a couple miles of private beach, acres of marsh— ducks, geese, quail, pheasants, rabbits, foxes, and deer, fresh garden produce, fish, crabs, and oysters. For anyone who loved to hunt and fish, it *was* paradise, and it was ours. Even then we knew that we were very lucky, because we weren't rich. My father paid for his first shotgun by trapping muskrats; he borrowed money for college. We were the beneficiaries of our great-grandfather's courage and Colonel Dulaney's gratitude. Simple as that.

The older I got, the farther I traveled, the stronger that farm pulled on me. It never pulled harder than when I lived in the Pacific Northwest, the most famously beautiful part of the country, with its lakes and the Puget Sound surrounded by majestic snow-capped peaks. The Puget Sound is a beautiful, useful body of water. Ferries travel over it; salmon migrate through it. The Sound forms a glorious backdrop for the city of Seattle, a gorgeous foreground for the Olympic Mountains. But it is also deep and cold; there's no Continental Shelf out west. The shoreline slopes steeply to the ocean floor. There's no Gulf Stream either; the Puget and Pacific are frigid even in July.

The Chesapeake is not majestic; its shoreline is flat and featureless; many of its waters are too shallow for navigation. But its waters are very fertile; they teem with life, a biologic porridge, the greatest estuary on earth, compared to which the Puget Sound is a sterile, deep, marine desert. Unfair, of course. It doesn't matter. These things don't lend themselves to rational analysis any more than, say, love does. Some places simply match our unconscious templates of home and paradise, and some don't.

So, after several years in Seattle, I didn't pull up roots as much as I was pulled up by my roots and dragged back to that farm beside the Chesapeake. I knew, everyone knows, "you can't go home again," but technically Kilmarnock had never been my home. It had been a refuge, a sanctuary, but not home; therefore, I thought I could safely go there. I was wrong. After all, what is home if not a refuge or sanctuary?

But already the place was changed almost beyond recognition. Many of the older generation had died off in a few short years. Two of the three "old home places" were empty. My cousin Hal occupied the third alone. The next generation was building new houses for vacation or retirement. The place hardly resembled a farm anymore. The animals were gone; the hedgerows had been cleaned up and plowed under; fields were clipped as short as fairways; quail were disappearing. The commercial fishing industry was dying out too, and the bay was being taken over by pleasure boats, sportfishermen. There wasn't a single fish trap to be seen in the entire Dividing Creek area, just crab pots and gill nets, neither of which were popular with the sporting crowd. Gill nets killed fish, and crab pot lines snagged careless boaters.

In moving back, not only had I not cured my homesickness; I had added another layer. Now I missed the Northwest, its mountains, lakes, the cool rainy weather, the urban pleasures of Seattle. I missed friends, and I missed the anonymity of city life, the way a person could lose himself in the interstices of the city. I now felt as exposed as a quail whose honeysuckle-covered hiding places had been obliterated. My sanctuary was gone, and I knew it was gone for good.

There was nothing to do but move—again—this time across the Bay to the Eastern Shore—with water on both sides. But the house was rented and, therefore, could not be home. On the other hand, it sat hard by the Chesapeake in the middle of a huge field, one year planted in asparagus, the next year sweet corn. We raided each equally. In winter a cover crop of wheat attracted enormous flocks of wary geese. They'd come in very high and spiral down, a funnel cloud of geese that unfortunately offered little opportunity for the hunter. The western edge of the field dropped twenty feet straight down to a skinny strip of beach, then the Bay. But having that Bay to the west was disorienting: the sun was supposed to *rise* over the Bay, not set. Those were the rules.

Next came Maine, another coastal state. My first home there was in the woods, no water except a fishless trickle of stream. Then, eight years ago, I bought this place on Lovejoy Pond. I'd never wanted to live on the water in Maine. Property taxes were too high, and most ponds offered public access anyway, but once I looked at the place on Lovejoy Pond, something kept pulling me back. That something, of course, was the water. The idea of having fish in my front yard outweighed all other rational, financial considerations. So I bought the place.

It is rural but not remote, and it isn't paradise. Four months a year the pond is frozen solid. In July and August powerboats and the dreaded jet skis churn and whine and keep the water in constant turmoil—except in the early mornings, which even in midsummer are tranquil and mostly mine. Like the wildlife, I sneak my pleasures in around the edges: early mornings; before Memorial Day and after Labor Day; and even in the winter, when the water's frozen over, crusted with snow, which offers good traction for walking. From my living room window, I've seen moose, deer, foxes, mink, beavers, mergansers, goldeneyes, herons, ospreys, loons, hawks, owls, and eagles. The oak trees bring wood ducks and teal to the shallows for acorns; sometimes they even feed in the yard. One night I watched a young fox chase my cat across the yard, and a few moments later, as in a cartoon, my cat chased the fox back the other way. But birds and mammals were not the creatures that drew me to Lovejoy Pond. Fish were.

The window of my office faces the lake. The water is often dimpled with feeding sunfish and bass. From my office I've watched smallmouth bass rise to flying ants, and two minutes later I would be casting to the same bass from my canoe. That's the beauty of living on the water; it's what makes the property tax bearable. When nature calls, in the form of rising fish, I can answer immediately. And I do. And sometimes I have to meet nature and the fish halfway; I have to be on the water, ready to receive the call, just in case.

I still make regular visits to the farm on the Chesapeake. I want my boys to know and love it, because it is still a wonderful place. It's just not the same wonderful place I knew in my child-hood. It's a different wonderful place, the place my children knew in their childhood, and now their early adulthood, changing before their very eyes, same as always. The farm's contours are in a state of flux. The same warming trend that has moderated Maine winters is raising the sea level and eroding our low-lying farm-land. The place is literally shrinking.

When we visit the farm, we stay in the "new" house my father built in 1981, shortly before he died, his retirement dreams cut short by pancreatic cancer. The house is a low, brick, one-story structure—simple, functional, nothing fancy—on a wooded point my father inherited from his father. My father's musty old medical texts still line the shelves, which they share with a porce-lain Irish setter, a stuffed quail, my brother's broken sports tro-phies, a ship model, and fading photographs. The living room is like a museum whose exhibits never change, because no one stays there long enough to change them. But now my nearly grown children infuse the place with life and youthful enthusiasm and their plans for the place. It's an important part of their lives. My father would have liked that.

On a recent visit, I was sitting in the living room, sipping cof-fee, looking out on Jarvis Creek, when it hit me how the view from that house was almost identical to the view from my place on Lovejoy Pond. It was remarkable really, and I'd never noticed it before. One place was beside fresh water, the other beside salt, but the similarities were striking: the distance from the water, which lay to the east (the proper side); the mix of softwood and oak; the yard of leaves and pine needles; the wildlife; and the land visible across the water. I hadn't consciously thought of it when I bought the house in Maine, but it was more than a coincidence.

The truth was, I couldn't leave home even if I tried. My con-cept of home was carried in my genes, like the color of my hair and eyes. I couldn't escape home any more than I could disavow my blood type. In a way, it was a relief. My father and I did not see eye to eye on much of anything. He was civil about it, but the fact was, he basically disapproved of how I lived my life, and he took his disapproval to his grave. That was part of his legacy. So it was nice to realize, belatedly, that even though my life didn't please him, at least he would have liked the view.